AMISH HOUSES & BARNS

STEPHEN SCOTT

A People's Place Book

Good Books

Intercourse, PA 17534

Acknowledgements

All photography by Stephen E. Scott except pp. 2, 3, 6, 10 and 11 (top and bottom) by Beth Oberholtzer, p. 5 (lower right and lower left) by Kenneth Pellman and author photo, pg. 158 by Dawn J. Ranck. Front cover by Doyle Yoder and back cover by Kenneth Pellman.

AMISH HOUSES AND BARNS

Design by Dawn J. Ranck

Library of Congress Cataloging-in-Publication Data

Scott, Stephen, 1948-
    Amish houses and barns / Stephen Scott.
        p. cm.
    "A People's Place book."
    ISBN 1-56148-052-5
    1. Amish—United States—Social life and customs. 2. Farm life—United States. 3. Dwellings—United States. 4. Barns—United States. 5. Agriculture—United States. 6. United States—Social life and customs.
Title. II. Title: People's Place book.
E184.M45S35 1992
973' .088287-dc20   92-28090
                                                                CIP

Table of Contents

1.
Home:
The Center of Amish Life

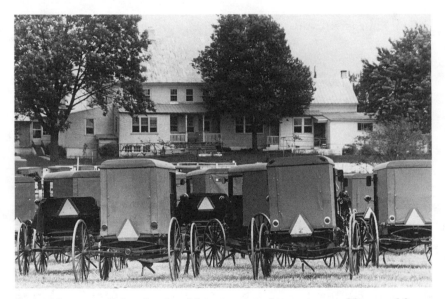

In Amish society all church-related functions-worship services, weddings and funerals—occur in the home. Many Amish people also prefer that both birth and death take place at home.

The Old Order Amish have no church buildings, no recreation halls, no nursing homes and no funeral parlors. All the functions of these facilities normally take place in their homes. The Amish world revolves around the home.

Although hospitals and modern medicine are used by the Amish people when needed, many Amish women also prefer the warm, familiar surroundings of home for giving birth. Registered midwives and doctors who agree to make home deliveries are patronized. In some Amish communities doctors provide rural, home-like birthing centers for their Amish clients.

Most Amish people also prefer to spend their last days in the familiar home environment. Every effort is made to preserve life (although not artificially prolong it), but when death seems imminent an Amish person will usually choose to be with the family at home. While the deceased person is taken to a mortuary for preparation, the body comes back to the home for the viewing and funeral.

Togetherness At All Costs

As the institution of the home crumbles in North America the Amish take great effort to preserve it. Many of the radical nonconformist practices of

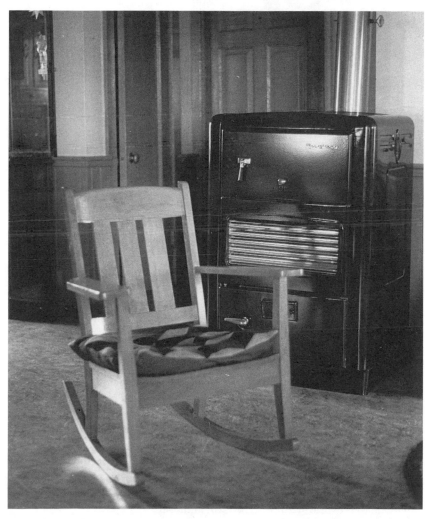

Limited technology in Amish homes is conducive to family togetherness. Space heaters draw family members together. The ban on cars also helps to keep people at home.

In Amish society three or more generations of a family often live on the same farmstead. The Dawdy Haus *(grandfather house) makes the elderly an integral part of the family unit.*

Amish life were instituted to nurture family cohesiveness. The whole idea of restricting mobility by forbidding the ownership of cars is an endeavor to preserve home life. Amish people argue that fast, easy transportation draws family members away from the home.

Limited technology within the home further draws the family together and discourages the isolation of individual members. The lack of central heating promotes family togetherness in the few heated rooms in the house. Prohibiting electricity and restricting the number of light sources encourages family life by fostering a central place where all family members spend time reading, working on hobbies or playing games.

The Elderly: Needed and Wanted

The Amish also try to keep the elderly involved in the life of the home. Typically, a small separate house or an addition to the larger house will be built for the grandparents after their children have families of their own. This is the classic *Dawdy Haus* (grandfather house). In wisdom these quarters have their own kitchens and the grandparents usually do all of their own food preparation. The Amish realize that parent-child relationships can be strained by the continual presence of grandparents. However, the aged are highly respected and made to feel useful around the farm and home.

While an Amish farmer generally hands over responsibility for the farm to the younger generation earlier than normal retirement age, he does not really retire. His help around the farm is both essential and welcome. Often the older family will start a small cottage industry to occupy their time and provide some extra income.

Home: The Place of Work

Younger families have also increasingly turned to cottage industries as farmland has become scarce and expensive. These home businesses make it possible for young Amish men to stay at home with their families. They work together

As farmland has become scarce and expensive in the larger Amish communities, many families have turned to a variety of cottage industries. Like farming, members of the family can work together. Some of these home businesses provide for the unique needs of the Amish while others cater to outsiders.

with their wives and children in much the same way as they would on a farm. Buggy shops, harness shops, woodworking shops, dry goods stores and many other businesses typically involve the labor of many members of the family. Many Amish mothers also supplement the family income by producing quilts and other crafts in the home. With the exception of occasional help from Grossmommy next-door, no day care is needed.

Home: The Place of Worship

Individual Amish families are directly involved with the life of the church because they take turns hosting worship services in their homes. Each Amish congregation consists of a geographical unit called a district which typically includes from twenty to forty family units. Worship services are held every other Sunday in most Amish communities; thus, a turn comes around no more than once or twice a year. By focusing on the home as the place of worship, the church in Amish society is thought of as a body of believers rather than a building or a place. Each family contributes to the life of the church by providing both a place for meeting and the food for a fellowship meal after the services.

Much preparation precedes an Amish church service. The family spends many hours cleaning the house, sprucing up the farmstead and preparing food. The furniture is removed from several rooms in the house and simple, backless benches are arranged in closely spaced rows. Some of these same benches are transformed into dinner tables after the church service.

Each family in an Amish church district takes its turn hosting a church service. Specially designed wagons transport the church benches from one home to the next. In warm weather church services are often held in barns.

Home: The Place of Recreation

On a different level, the home is also the scene of evening social activities among Amish young people. Traditionally, unmarried young folks have gathered around tables in living rooms and kitchens to sing hymns on Sunday evenings. Depending on the mind-set of the particular youth group, the gatherings occasionally are not so docile.

Courtship also takes place at home. A young Amish man typically has a date at his girlfriend's home after the Sunday evening singing. In some communities Saturday night is also a time for dating. Although the dating couples meet in the home, they are normally secluded from other members of the family, spending their time together in the formal parlor after the rest of the family has gone to bed.

One of the few major functions of life that does not take place in the home is school. However, even in this case the schools are small, one-room buildings maintained and managed by the Amish community. They are usually within walking distance of every student's home.

2.
Amish Architecture

The absence of electric lines and the presence of a long washline and horse barn indicate Amish ownership of this Lancaster County home even though the house appears quite modern.

When traveling through Amish communities, one may notice certain distinctive architectural features. In addition, individual Amish communities sometimes also have their own unique architectural styles. For example, Amish farmsteads in LaGrange County, Indiana, have some features which distinguish them quite clearly from Amish farmsteads in Lancaster County, Pennsylvania.

However, uniformity in architectural styles holds far less importance in the Amish world than uniformity in dress and vehicle styles. Through the years building styles appear to have changed more than most other areas of Amish life. In addition to terrain and available materials, the lack of complete uniformity in building styles is affected by the fact that Amish people moving into new communities often buy houses built by non-Amish people. While they usually modify the buildings to suit their needs, the core structures remain. These hybrid structures sometimes influence later new structures on Amish homesteads. The Amish have also copied architectural features from their "English" neighbors. This has especially been true in recent years when many Amish carpenters have been employed as homebuilders for the larger society. Ideas picked up while building houses for non-Amish people are sometimes used when constructing homes for themselves.

Although architecture is not as uniform as many areas of Amish life, each community has developed some unique building styles. The farm in the top photograph shows a multi-generation house and large white barn characteristic of Lancaster County, Pennsylvania. The farm in the bottom photograph shows a distinctively simple house and unpainted barn particular to the "white top" Amish of central Pennsylvania.

The Amish have been accused of overemphasizing externals, but where architectural styles are concerned, outward appearances in some respects appear unimportant. Many older houses especially lack any semblance of exterior symmetry. Even when Amish people move into houses built along classic Georgian lines, the original form is eventually obscured by numerous additions jutting from all sides of the structure. It appears many Amish families give little

(top) This Amish home near Aylmer, Ontario, demonstrates the Amish emphasis on simplicity and the disregard for symmetry in respect to the placement of windows.

(bottom) Kitchens in many Amish homes look surprisingly modern. This Lancaster County example shows how a family can live quite comfortably without electricity. There is hot and cold running water, a gas stove and a gas refrigerator. A gas mantle lamp hangs over the table.

thought to presenting a unified architectural facade to passersby. In fact, it is often difficult to tell which door represents the main entrance to an Amish house.

Appearance of Amish Homes

When designing new homes or additions to an existing structure, the practicality of the interior arrangement is valued above outward form. Stories are told of houses being built from plans drawn on the back of used envelopes. Windows of various sizes are placed here and there, depending on where they

Ornamentation is kept at a minimum inside Amish homes. A cupboard filled with fancy dishes and a bookcase containing a few knickknacks are permissible in many communities. Paintings or photographs on the walls are generally forbidden unless accompanied by a calendar.

Amish pioneers in the 18th century probably lived in houses similar to this one. The fireplace was near the center of early Pennsylvania German houses rather than on a gable end like those of English speaking people. The interior featured a traditional three-room plan. (Landis Valley Museum)

are needed without regard to exterior balance.

The interiors of many Amish homes look quite modern. Most kitchens in the Lancaster County Amish community, for example, have finely made kitchen cabinets and hot and cold running water. Pumps operate with compressed air and water heaters use propane gas. Conventional looking refrigerators and kitchen ranges also operate on propane gas. One obvious absence in Amish homes is electric lights. In their place are various kinds of kerosene or gasoline burning lamps. Space heaters which burn wood, coal, kerosene or propane replace central heating units. Linoleum floors are typical, but wall-to-wall carpet is rare, indeed without vacuum sweepers it is quite impractical. Old-fashioned rag carpets are still produced in some Amish communities, including Lancaster County.

There is a general lack of decoration in Amish homes but a *Schank* (cupboard) with glass doors may display fancy dishes and knickknacks. Framed pictures are taboo, especially those showing people, but calendars with pictures are usually acceptable.

Because of the autonomous nature of church government in Amish congregations, rules regarding the appearances of homes vary considerably from one Amish community to the next and even from one congregation to the next in the same community. The most conservative Amish communities and groups have more definite standards on matters pertaining to houses than do the moderate majority of Amish people. The ultra-conservative Amish often require very spartan living quarters. Indoor bathrooms, hot water heaters and modern-style kitchen cabinets are proscribed by these groups. Cookstoves usually must be black and burn wood or coal only. No patterned material of any kind may be used on the walls and floors. In a few Amish groups no rugs or carpets are used at all.

Among these more conservative groups, exterior appearances are often also regulated more carefully. For example, siding on the houses must be white and shingles may not be two-toned. The Swartzentruber Amish of Holmes and Wayne Counties in Ohio, one of the most conservative groups, specify that windows shall have six panes in each sash. Some slightly less conservative midwestern Amish communities specify that windows should have four panes in each half or six panes in one part and two in the other. Since windows with large panes of glass are a fairly recent innovation, these rules are probably meant to keep the houses from appearing too modern. For the same reason doors and storm doors with large panes of glass are not permitted in some communities. Most Amish churches make no specifications about window panes. However, most do discourage the use of large picture windows which cannot be opened. Two windows beside each other create nearly the same effect on some Amish homes but these "twin windows" are also prohibited in some communities.

Practices relating to curtains vary a great deal from one community to the next. In Lancaster County dark green window blinds are the general rule. In Holmes County the more conservative districts insist on simple one-piece curtains (not divided in the middle) made of dark blue or black cloth. In Geauga County, Ohio, and Lawrence County, Pennsylvania, white curtains are the norm.

The 1719 Herr house is a classic example of the Flürkuchenhaus. *It was built by Mennonite pioneers in Lancaster County, Pennsylvania.*

The pervasive English Georgian-style house eventually was adopted by many Pennsylvania Germans. A derivative of this style was known as a "four over four" house because of its eight-room arrangement with a central hallway. Many Amish homes are modified Georgian types.

Pioneer Pennsylvania German Houses

It is apparent that Amish people today live in homes quite different than those they built on their arrival in North America in the 1700s. During the first three-quarters of the 18th century, Pennsylvania German settlers employed a distinctive architectural style which was probably also common among the Amish. This house type has been known as the Continental-style house (because of its supposed origin in Europe), the Pennsylvania German central chimney house or the corridor-kitchen house, a term which describes one of its architectural features. The German term for corridor-kitchen house, *Flürkuchenhaus*, is the generally accepted nomenclature used by many current architectural historians. The most famous and one of the few surviving examples of this house style is the 1719 Herr House built by some of the first Mennonite settlers in Lancaster County, Pennsylvania.

The first floor of a typical 18th century Pennsylvania German house featured a central fireplace with three or four rooms situated around it. The open area of the large fireplace naturally was in the *Küch*, (kitchen). The main, and often only, entrance to the house opened into the *Küch*. The closed stairways to the second floor and the basement usually were also entered from the *Küch*.

Unlike the early settlers from the British Isles, the Pennsylvania Germans did not eat and socialize around the hearth. The practical Germans sacrificed the romance of the open fire for the efficiency of stoves long before Ben Franklin. An early Pennsylvania German stove consisted of a brick or cast-iron box extending from the fireplace into the opposite room. A fire built in this

(top) *This house was built about 1810 for Amishman Christian Fisher Jr. The offset door and three-room arrangement are traditional Pennsylvania German features. The gable-end fireplace, however, shows English influence.*

(bottom) *A style known as the Pennsylvania farmhouse features two front doors. One explanation for this practice is that the one door enters the kitchen while the other is used only for the formal living room or parlor.*

15

stove provided even heat with low fuel consumption to the room opposite the fireplace. This was known as the *Stube* in High German or *Schtupp* in Pennsylvania German, which originally meant "stove room." The real life of the family took place in this room—eating, visiting, domestic crafts and, occasionally, even sleeping.

A downstairs bedroom was called a *Kammer* (chamber) and was usually reserved for the father and mother of the house. Sometimes part of the stove in the *Schtupp* was shared with the *Kammer*. The *Kammerli* was a smaller room found in some houses which served as a bedroom, storage room or pantry.

The distinctive style of this Pennsylvania German house was gradually replaced by a roomier Georgian style of English origin. Georgian houses featured four nearly equal-sized rooms divided by a central hallway containing stairs to the upper floor which also had four rooms. The classic Georgian-style house found in Pennsylvania had a symmetrical facade with two windows on either side of a central door and five corresponding windows on the second floor. Each gable end had a built-in chimney in the center, two windows on the first floor and two corresponding windows on the second floor.

There were numerous variations of the Georgian theme. One style found among Pennsylvania Germans appears to have been a combination of the Georgian house and the Pennsylvania *Flürkuchenhaus*. Authorities disagree as to the origin of this style. It has been variously known as a Quaker-plan house, a two-thirds Georgian house or a Continental deep house. The interior arrangement of this style featured three rooms and an offset entrance like the *Flürkuchenhaus*, but the fireplace was on one of the gable ends rather than in the center of the house.

One surviving example of this hybrid style in Lancaster County, Pennsylvania, possibly preserves an early example of Amish architecture (see photo, p. 15). This small, one-and-a-half story, stuccoed, stone house has a three-room interior arrangement like the *Flürkuchenhaus* but the fireplace is situated in one of the gable ends. The single offset doorway opens into the hearth room. According to tradition, this was the first home of Christian Fisher Jr. (1789-1874), an early Amish immigrant, and his bride Fanny Stoltzfus (1793-1817). It stands on land owned by Christian Fisher Sr. between 1790 and 1812. Even though the house was probably only occupied by Christian and Fanny for less than two years, because the Fisher clan moved further west in Lancaster County, it is significant because of its traditional Pennsylvania German architecture. It is unlikely that any significant changes were made when the house was moved a short distance from its original location in 1877. It has fallen into considerable disrepair on an otherwise prospering Lancaster County farm.

Another common house structure found in the Pennsylvania German area also combines traditional German and Georgian features. The exteriors of these houses look basically Georgian but the interiors retain the German three-room plan. Sometimes called the Pennsylvania farmhouse by architectural historians, many of these houses employ the curious practice of having two side-by-side front doors. Scholars have long theorized about the purpose of two front doors. One explanation suggests that one door served as an everyday entrance to the kitchen while the other opened into the formal living room or parlor. In this way special visitors could be taken directly into the best part of the house without going through the more lived-in quarters. A Lancaster County Amishman called the extra door a "boyfriend door" because young men traditionally avoided confrontations with their girlfriends' families by using the separate door to the parlor where evening dates customarily took place.

While the Amish have adopted more modern styles of architecture, the words used to describe rooms in the *Flürkuchenhaus* still persist. The *Küch* is still the kitchen, but is much larger and has come to include the dining area and often an informal living area as well. *Schtupp* no longer means "stove room," but is now often preceded by a descriptive adjective such as *gut Schtupp* (good room) or *schlof Schtupp* (sleep room). *Kammer* still designates a downstairs bedroom for the parents in the family.

The *Dawdy Haus*

A distinguishing feature on the farmsteads of many Amish communities is the presence of a *Dawdy Haus* (grandfather house). These structures provide living quarters for the grandparents of the family who have gone into semi-retirement and relinquished the major responsibility of the farm to the younger generation. It is not unusual to find three or four generations of an Amish family living on the same farmstead.

The *Dawdy Haus* takes many different forms. In Lancaster County it is usually an addition to the house. Frequently, there are two additions to Lancas-

Many Amish homes have several additions providing space for three or more generations. Sometimes the Dawdy Haus *(grandfather house) is a separate unit.*

Flürkuchenhaus
(The 1719 Herr House)

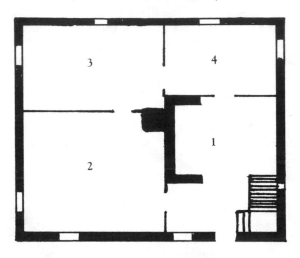

1. Küch (Kich)
2. Stube (Schtupp)

3. Kammer
4. Kammerli

Holmes County Amish House ca. 1920s

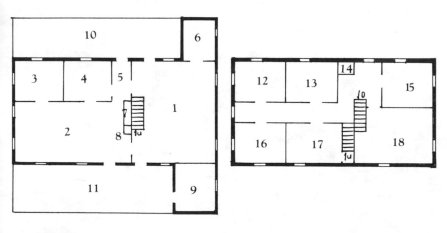

FIRST FLOOR
1. Kitchen
2. Sitting room
3. Bedroom
4. Bedroom
5. Hall
6. Pantry
7. Closet

8. Medicine Cabinet
9. Storage
10. Open porch
11. Open porch

SECOND FLOOR
12. Bedroom
13. Bedroom
14. Closet
15. Bedroom
16. Bedroom
17. Storage room
18. Bedroom

18

1880-1950 Lancaster Amish House

(according to Samuel S. Stoltzfus)

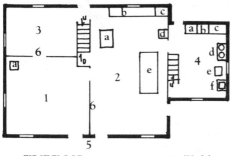
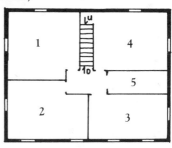

FIRST FLOOR
1. Parlor (formal living room)
   a. stove
2. Kitchen
   a. range
   b. sink
   c. ice box
   d. cabinet
   e. table
3. *Kammer* (parent's bedroom)

4. Wash house
   a. coal
   b. wood
   c. privy
   d. kettle stove
   e. washing machine
   f. sink
5. Open porch
6. Removable partition

SECOND FLOOR
1. Good room
2. Bedroom
3. Bedroom
4. Hired help room
5. Closet (used to bathe in winter)

1960-1990 Lancaster Amish House

(according to Samuel S. Stoltzfus)

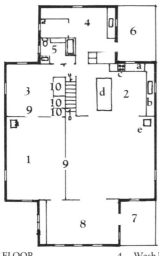
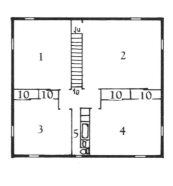

FIRST FLOOR
1. Parlor
   a. stove
2. Kitchen
   a. range
   b. sink
   c. refrigerator
   d. table
   e. stove
3. *Kammer* (parent's bedroom)

4. Wash house
   a. washing machine
5. Bathroom
6. Open porch
7. Open porch
8. Enclosed porch
   a. cabinet
9. Removable partition
10. Closet

SECOND FLOOR
1. Bedroom
2. Bedroom
3. Bedroom
4. Bedroom
5. Bathroom

The traditional Pennsylvania barn featured an overhanging second level above the first level stable entrances. An earthen bank provided a ground level entrance to the second level.

ter County Amish houses, creating a unique stair-step effect. In Holmes County, Ohio, the *Dawdy Haus* is more often a separate unattached dwelling. In LaGrange County, Indiana, both forms are fairly common.

Pennsylvania Barns

The Amish represent a small part of a broader culture known as the Pennsylvania Dutch or the Pennsylvania Germans. One of the most visible and widespread contributions of this culture to the American landscape is the Pennsylvania barn. Scholars debate the origin of this barn style. A number of architectural historians have concluded it is the product of several European traditions blending in the New World. Robert Ensminger, an expert on barn architecture, has accumulated considerable evidence showing that the Pennsylvania barn descends from the distinctive barn styles of central and northeastern Switzerland. Indeed, the structure of Pennsylvania barns is quite similar to the Swiss barns, and in some old documents the Pennsylvania buildings in question are called "Swisser" or "Sweitzer" barns.

The Pennsylvania barn is of the "bank" barn type. While the Pennsylvania bank barn is usually much larger than other bank barns, it shares many characteristics with other bank barns. A two-story structure with earth banked up to the second level on the back side, this barn style has ground level entrances to both floors. Hay and straw are stored in mows and lofts on either side of a large middle section, traditionally called the threshing floor. The first floor of the barn contains stables for cows, horses and other animals. The Pennsylvania bank barn's most distinguishing feature is the "forebay," an extension of the

Outdoor bake ovens were present on many Pennsylvania German farms. A few of the most conservative Amish still make use of similar ovens to bake in quantity. However, in most Amish homes the regular cookstove oven generally suffices. The back of this building served as a smoke house to cure meat. (Landis Valley Museum)

Other Farm Buildings

A Pennsylvania German farm in the 1800s typically contained a variety of buildings in addition to the house and barn. One of the most common of the outbuildings was a summer house or summer kitchen. In the days when cooking was done in an open fireplace or on a wood- or coal-burning cookstove, the heat generated by the cooking fire was unwelcome on sultry summer days. To avoid heating up the main house a separate, smaller building was constructed for summer cooking. Quite often this summer kitchen was actually the original house on a farm which had been occupied until a larger house could be built to accommodate an expanding family. Summer houses are still frequently seen and used on Amish farms. In Holmes County, Ohio, families customarily move to cooler quarters in the basement of the house during the summer months.

In pioneer days the presence of a spring was a strong selling point for a plot of land. Buildings were usually built over the spring and channels were contructed for the water to flow through. The cool water was used for natural refrigeration for food. The spring house was often a very small structure, but frequently also was large enough to serve as the first dwelling house on the farm. Later, when a larger house was built, the spring house doubled as a summer house. Spring houses are still found on many Amish farms. Among the most conservative Amish, the cool water is still the only source of refrigeration.

Smoke houses and bake houses are two types of buildings common on 19th century farms which are rarely found among the Amish today. Few Amish people cure their own meat and baking is done in the regular family cookstove oven.

A building obsolete in the larger society, but still quite useful to the Amish, is the wash house. While some Amish homes use the basement as a laundry room, a separate small building called a wash house is still quite common. Originally, these houses contained a pump or other source of water and a stove for heating water. The old-style stove was made of bricks and had built-in iron kettles on the top. The kettles could also be used for preparing large quantities of food and for butchering. In the old days the wash house might also contain a bake oven.

In addition to the main barn a number of other buildings to shelter animals may be found on an Amish farm. On the traditional diversified farm small houses for a few chickens and hogs were commonplace. In recent years large specialized hog and poultry operations with their distinctive long pole barns have appeared on Amish farms.

Descriptions of Amish Farmsteads
in Lancaster County in 1815

The 1815 Direct Tax list contains descriptions of buildings on Lancaster County properties. The details are limited to size and building materials, but the information helps to identify the physical appearance of farmsteads. This chart was created by first isolating properties owned by people with typical Amish surnames. Those names were then cross-referenced with the comprehensive data in *Amish and Amish Mennonite Genealogies* (Gingerich and Kreider, 1986) to establish whether Amish people with the names indicated were actually living in Lancaster County at the time of the 1815 direct tax.

Leacock Township

Christian King - 140 acres, 2 story log house 30x24, 1 stone barn, 1 log barn, weaver shop, 1 corn and waggon house, 1 log tennant house and stable. Value - $12,200.

Joseph Lapp - 32 acres, 1 story wood house (old), 1 log barn. Value - $3,000.

John Lapp Jr. - 130 acres, 2 story stone house 40x30, 1 stone barn, 1 stone kitchen, 1 tennant house of logs. Value - $12,850.

David Stulsfooz - 94 acres, 2 story wood house 30x32, 1 stone barn, 1 story stone tennant house. Value - $8,690.

Abraham Stulsfooz - 94 acres, 1 story log house 30x18, 1 barn of frame. Value - $8,400.

John Stulsfooz - 130 acres, 2 story brick house 30x28, 1 brick barn, 1 brick kitchen. Value - $11,800.

Christian Stulsfooz - 94 acres, 2 story log house 30x30, 1 wood barn. Value - $8,690.

Christian Zook Jr. - 95 acres, 2 story wood house 26x18, 1 stone barn, 1 log kitchen. Value - $8,600.

Christian Zook Sr. - 110 acres, 2 story log house 26x19, 1 stone barn, 1 log kitchen, corn and waggon house (barn). Value - $9,600.

Lampeter Township

John Beiler - 155 acres, 1 story log house 23x17, 1 old barn. Value - $13,355.

David Beiler - 100 acres, 2 story log house 29x27, stone barn 70x35. Value - $9,100.

Jonathan Beiler - 75 acres, 2 story stone house 44x30, frame barn 60x30, 1 story log tennant house 19x19. Value - $7,275.

John King Sr. - 57 acres, 2 story stone house 26x26, stone barn 40x30. Value - $5,595.

John King (turnpike) - 141 acres, 2 story log house 30x26, 1 stone barn 70x35, 1 story log tennant house 25x24, 1 story log tennant house 24x20. Value - $12,935.

Isaac Lapp - 78 acres, 2 story log house 34x27, frame barn 90x30. Value - $7,380.

Isaac Lapp (Soudersburg) - 86 perches, 1 story brick 22x19. Value - $335.

Michael Lapp Sr. (Soudersburg) - 120 perches, 1 story log house 20x19. Value -$500.

Jacob Lantz - 16 acres, 2 story log house 26x24, 1 stable, 1 story log tennant house 24x22. Value - $2,000.

Abraham Zook - 150 acres, 2 story brick house 40x21, frame barn 80x30, 2 story mill house of brick 50x30. Value - $17,750.

Strasburg Township

Christian Fisher Sr. - 83 acres, 2 story brick house 24x34, 1 stone barn 70x35, 1 brick kitchen. Value - $9,310.

Christian Fisher Jr. - 83 acres, 2 story brick house 30x30, 1 barn part stone 70x35. Value - $9,310.

Jacob Yoder - 87 acres, 2 story stone house 28x18, stone barn 65x35. Value - $9,600.

John Yoder - 110 acres, 2 story stone house 30x28, stone barn 60x30, 1 oil mill frame. Value - $12,750.

Caernarvon Township

Christian Hartzler Sr. - 37 acres in the valley and 44 acres in the forest, 1 story stone house 30x16, 1 stone barn. Value - $4,300.

Daniel Hartzler - 100 acres and 24 acres in the forest, 1 story log house 20x18, 1 stone barn, 1 stone still house. Value - $5,000.

Christian Hartzler Jr. - 143 acres in the valley and 86 acres in the forest, 2 story stone house 30x30, 1 barn of stone and logs, 1 story tennant house of logs. Value - $11,900.

Stephen Kaufman - 170 acres, 2 story stone house 34x30, 1 barn of stone. Value - $10,600.

John Zook - 150 acres, 1 story stone and log house 18x20, stone barn. Value- $10,600.

Summary Of Materials And Dimensions
Lancaster Amish Buildings,1815

HOUSES

LOG		STONE	
One-story	Two-story	One-story	Two-story
23x17	30x24	30x16	40x30
30x18	30x30	20 x 18 (part log)	44x30
20x19	26x19		26x26
20x18	29x27		28x18
	30x26		30x30
	34x27		34x30
	26x24		

BRICK		FRAME	
One-story	Two-story	One-story	Two-story
22x19	30x28		30x32
	40x21		36x18
	24x34		
	30x30		
	30x28		

BARNS

LOG	STONE
1 unmeasured	9 unmeasured
	70x35
	40x30
	70x35
	70x35
	70x35
	65x35 (part stone)
	60x30

BRICK	FRAME
1 unmeasured	2 unmeasured
	60x30
	90x30
	80x30

3

The Lancaster County, Pennsylvania, Amish Community

The main Lancaster County Amish settlement is called the Pequea after the creek that runs through the center of the community. The Pequea settlement began about 1790. Several other earlier communities eventually either became extinct or merged with the Pequea group.

Lancaster County, Pennsylvania, is the best known of all Amish communities. It is certainly the oldest continuously occupied Amish settlement in North America, and may in fact be the oldest Amish settlement. Berks County has long been considered the home of the first Amish community in the New World. Evidence exists, however, that two Amish settlements began in Lancaster County near the same time and, perhaps, even earlier than the Berks County Amish community.

Known as the Cocalico and Old Conestoga settlements, these two places

Lancaster Amish farms usually have a number of buildings in addition to the house and barn.

were located in the northern part of Lancaster County. Amish people had settled the Old Conestoga area by 1737, about the same time Amish established themselves in Berks County. The Cocalico settlement may have started a few years earlier, but some historians question whether the people at Cocalico were actually Amish. At any rate, by the early 1800s both the Berks County settlement and the Cocalico settlement were extinct.

The date 1760 is often given as the beginning of the Lancaster Amish settlement. This was the approximate time when the Conestoga (not Old Conestoga) settlement began in the vicinity of Morgantown, Pennsylvania. However, it is highly probable that the Old Conestoga settlement was occupied by Amish from 1737 until at least 1790 which means Amish people have lived in Lancaster County since 1737.

Today the Amish people of Lancaster County refer to the area where they live as the Pequea, after the creek by that name. The first Amish came to the Pequea area in 1790 from Berks County, Pennsylvania. The Old Conestoga settlement was declining by this time and the remnant appear to have merged with the Pequea community.

As the Pequea community gradually expanded northward, the new Conestoga settlement also merged with the Pequea community. Another Amish congregation was started in the vicinity of Compass in eastern Lancaster County in the 1760s. These people also eventually were assimilated into the Pequea community.

The original Pequea Amish settlement was centered in Leacock Township near the current villages of Intercourse, Bird-in-Hand and Gordonville. In the

19th century Amish movement within Lancaster County was mainly to the east. During the 20th century, especially after 1940, the Lancaster Amish settlement expanded southward to the Maryland border. Since the 1960s there has been some growth toward the northwestern part of the county.

In 1900 there were six Amish church districts in Lancaster County. By 1925 there were eleven church districts, by 1950 there were twenty-six and by 1975 there were fifty-three, some of which extended into Chester County. By 1992 the rapidly growing Lancaster County community had ballooned to 103 church districts. Two districts in the Lancaster settlement which have been classed as New Order Amish since 1966 are included in this total.

(top) Lancaster Amish farms generally have less than 100 acres, large white barns and multi-generation houses.

(bottom) Most Lancaster Amish farmers are engaged in dairy farming. Corn and hay crops are used to feed the cows.

(top) The large structure near the center of the photo and to the right of the house is a tobacco barn. The main barn stands directly behind it. Tobacco leaves are hung in these structures to dry before being sold. An important cash crop since the 1800s, fewer Amish farmers grow tobacco each year.

(bottom) Many of the oldest Lancaster County barns have stone walls on the gable ends. Some of these were built by Amish but wood has been the main construction material for many years. Lancaster Amish barns usually have gable roofs (like the main barn) but recent barns nearly always feature gambrel or hip roofs (like the barn addition).

The open forebay on the traditional Pennsylvania bank barn is no longer common among Lancaster Amish. Although many Amish barns were originally built with the forebay, most have been modified through the years.

The buildings on both of these farms were constructed about 1990. The farm in the top picture is on the western fringe of the Lancaster Amish community. The one in the bottom picture is in the center of the Amish settlement. Note the remarkable similarity and uniformity along traditional lines.

(top) A number of Amish barns in Lancaster County have semi-gambrel roofs like this one. The cow barn roof has an unusual rounded roof style.

(bottom) Windmills and water wheels have traditionally been used to pump water on Lancaster Amish farms. However, these picturesque devices are being rapidly replaced by pneumatic pumps.

The units of a multi-generation house are usually joined only at one corner to allow for windows on all four sides of each unit. The resulting architecture presents a stair-step effect.

Since many young Amish men build houses for non-Amish people, current architectural trends often appear in the houses the Amish build for themselves. The houses in the photos on pages 38-39 are owned and occupied by Amish people.

(top) When an Amish family buys a house built by non-Amish people, they often add an enclosed porch. New Amish houses built in the traditional style almost always have these porches.

(bottom) Some recent Lancaster Amish houses are built of brick, but are still quite simple in style. The porch on the front of this house is temporarily enclosed, a common practice in Lancaster County at the time of a wedding. The special wagon parked in front of the porch transports church benches from one house to the next.

Many Lancaster Amish have been forced to engage in non-farm occupations because of the lack of available land. Various cottage industries are scattered through the community. Old wringer washing machines are renovated and sold from a shop on this Amish property.

4.
The Stoltzfus Farm of Lancaster County, Pennsylvania

The Stephen Stoltzfus farm occupies 52 acres in Leacock Township in Lancaster County, Pennsylvania. Amish people have lived here since 1827. The present farming operation concentrates on dairy cows and laying hens.

The Stephen Stoltzfus farm is located about midway between Bird-in-Hand and Intercourse in Leacock Township, Lancaster County, Pennsylvania. The farm's 52 acres contain an imposing, two-family house, a German-style bank barn, a long chicken house and an assortment of other large and small buildings. On the north the acreage borders Route 340, a busy two-lane highway, on the south a large orchard.

The farm was first occupied by European settlers about 1761 and has been in Amish ownership since 1825.

The Old Road

Today the busy highway going past the Stoltzfus farm is filled with fast-moving cars, along with the slower cars occupied by tourists eager for a glimpse of the many Old Order Amish people who live in Lancaster County. Special lanes

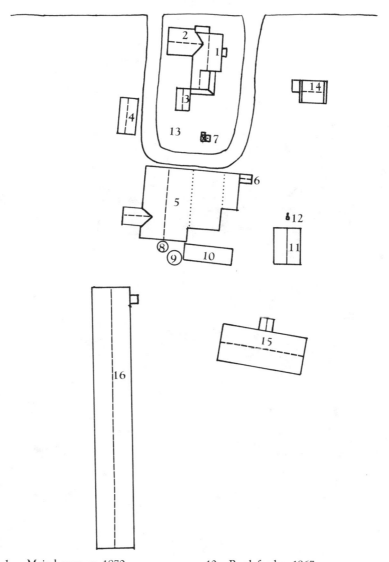

1. Main house - ca. 1870
2. *Dawdy Haus* - 1958
3. Wash house - moved to present location - ca. 1942
4. Buggy shed - 1970
5. Barn - 1908
6. Milk house - ca. 1942
7. Old milk house and windmill - 1920s
8. Silo (10 x 45) - 1930s
9. Silo (14 x 60) - 1972
10. Bunk feeder - 1967
11. Machinery shed - 1930s
12. Manure pump - 1986
13. Site of first chicken house - 1920s to 1972.
14. Chicken house - ca. 1942 (now used as buggy shed)
15. Chicken house - 1959 (now used for heifer pens)
16. Chicken house - 1975

(top) The oldest part of the Stoltzfus house (on the left) was probably built by Jacob Lapp in the early 1870s. Like the log structure it replaced, it stands quite close to the Old Philadelphia Pike.

(bottom) The east side of the house has two entrance doors. The door to the right (partially obscured by a shrub) probably was originally for the part of the house occupied by widow Elizabeth Lapp. Structural evidence indicates the northern section was at one time divided from the rest of the dwelling. A separate stairway led to the second floor.

(top) *The addition to the west side of the house (on the left) was built in 1958 as a Dawdy Haus. Christian and Emma Stoltzfus moved into this part when the newlyweds, Stephen and Nancy Stoltzfus, set up housekeeping in the main part of the house. Christian died in 1983 and Emma continued living here until 1987 when Stephen's son Daniel and his wife Anna Mary moved into the main house. Today, Stephen and Nancy live in the Dawdy Haus.*

(bottom) *Although electric lines have run past the Stoltzfus farm for about eighty years, no connection has ever been made to the flow of current.*

(top) The block wash house situated at a right angle to the enclosed porch was originally located further to the west. When Christian Stoltzfus moved onto the farm in 1942, the wash house was disassembled and attached to the house for convenience. The smokehouse and outhouse attachments on opposite ends of the original wash house were not rebuilt when the structure was moved.

(bottom) Originally, an open porch ran around the southeastern perimeter of the house. The eastern side was enclosed in the 1930s by Jacob Stoltzfus. In 1949 part of the southern side of the porch was enclosed and a bathroom installed. Eventually, in 1982 the entire porch was enclosed.

n once served to call hearing impaired Jacob
...es heard the bell and their behavior conveyed

...se-drawn vehicles of the Amish.
...he farm over two hundred years
...eat Conestoga wagons with their
...vas, the road became the main
...phia after its completion some-
...l Highway, it was renamed the
...ion. Despite the new name, the
...he drivers of Conestoga wagons
...uts and, on one particularly bad
...lled by the mud and dust.
...ke (now Route 30) was con-
...The old road was then often
...lly, the Old Philadelphia Pike.
...d Road."

...volutionary new idea—a roadbed of crushed
... America. The Old Road remained merely
...rs.

...peter Townships in Lancaster County are
...nish. This was not always the case since most
...e area were either Quakers or Presbyterians

47

(top) The
been mad
struck a
same bas

(bottom)
was built
original b

48

The shorter concrete silo, measuring 10 feet by 45 feet, was constructed by Jacob Stoltzfus, probably in the 1930s. It is believed an earlier wooden silo had been built between 1910 and 1915. The taller silo was built in 1972 and measures 14 feet by 60 feet. Both silos are unloaded by hand. The white mound in the foreground is called an "Ag Bag." This caterpillar-like silage container supplements the storage capacity of the silos.

from the British Isles.

The first owner of the land now occupied by the Stoltzfus farm was William Hamilton. After coming to America from Belfast, Ireland, Hamilton bought 200 acres of land in Leacock Township in 1745. He eventually amassed 1,400 acres, including a tract of 408 acres which he acquired through a government land patent on April 2, 1761. Hamilton prospered as a farmer and land agent and also owned the thriving Brick Tavern (formerly the Duke of Cumberland Inn) along the Old Philadelphia Pike. Two of the five Hamilton sons served in the Revolutionary War. William and his wife Jean (McMasters) Hamilton are buried at the Old Leacock Presbyterian Church cemetery about a mile east of the Stoltzfus farm.

On May 20, 1761, and only a month and a half after acquiring his 408-acre plot of government land, William Hamilton sold 100 acres, including the acreage which makes up the present-day Stoltzfus farm, to John Woods. John and Jane Woods and their twelve children were no doubt the first permanent residents of the farm. The Woods family cleared the land and constructed a log house and barn. However, they only stayed on the farm a short five years. On August 18, 1766, John and Jane Woods sold the property to their oldest son, George Woods. John Woods moved west with his family and died near Hano-

about 1770. George lived only six years longer than his father
idow, two sons and two daughters.

oods farm was sold in 1778 to John and Mary (or Molly)
30 acres to the southwest corner of the farm in 1785. Ten
9, 1795, John and Molly Henry sold their farm to Peter
re is known about the Henrys. Since no further records
ear in Lancaster County, we may assume they moved out

s probably Mennonite. Abraham, one of the Miller sons,
moved with a group of Mennonites to Waterloo County, Ontario, Canada in
1826. This Abraham Miller was born in York County, Pennsylvania, in 1769,
thus indicating the place of residence of the Miller family before they came to
Leacock Township. Another Miller son, Daniel, bought the Stoltzfus farm in
1802. Peter and Daniel Miller are buried at the Resh Cemetery next to the
present-day Weavertown Amish Mennonite Church. (This was a community
cemetery before the church was built.)

An Early Description of the Farm

In 1815 the struggling United States government levied a special tax to help
pay off debts accumulated during the War of 1812. Descriptions of the buildings on each landowner's property were required. According to this invaluable
record, the 1815 Daniel Miller farm contained 130 acres on which were found
"one two-story dwelling house of stone and logs measuring fifty feet by twenty-

*A bunk feeder was added in 1969 to accommodate the larger dairy herd. A wide roof
provides extra protection from the sun and rain while the cows feed.*

50

Timbers for the barn were floated down the Susquehanna River and milled in the river town of Marietta. Shipped by rail to the village of Ronks in 1908, they were transported by horse-drawn wagon to the building site. In earlier years the Stoltzfus barn occasionally became a rustic cathedral when church services were held in the large second floor area. The last religious gathering held there was the funeral of Christian Stoltzfus in 1983. Some Amish families still host services in the barn during the summer months.

five feet, one barn of stone, one corn and waggon house, and a one-story log tennant house." The property was valued at $11,700.

Most of the buildings had probably been built by John Woods fifty years earlier. Fifty years after 1815 a description of the buildings on the farm still read very much like the 1815 tax record. Evidently, this farm and its buildings remained relatively unchanged for almost 100 years.

Tennessee John Stoltzfus, The First Amish Occupant

In 1825 Michael Lapp became the first Amish owner of the land. However, he never lived on the property, having his own farm about a mile away, as the crow flies, near the present village of Ronks. In 1827 Lapp sold the farm to his brother-in-law John Stoltzfus. John had married Catharine Hooley in 1826, and they became the farm's first Amish occupants.

John Stoltzfus was born a mile southeast of Intercourse, Pennsylvania, along the Newport Road. His father, Jacob Stoltzfus (1779-1810), died when John was only four years old. Apparently widow Maria Blank Stoltzfus was unable to provide for the children because John and his three siblings were placed in the homes of relatives.

Catharine Hooley was born in the Mifflin County Amish settlement. Her parents had moved to Mifflin County in 1791 and were among the first Amish people to settle in that part of Pennsylvania. Catherine's father, John Hooley (1767-1857), was born in Lancaster County. Her mother, Elizabeth Mast (1776-1838), was born in Berks County.

These small enclosures originally served as granaries. They have not been used since about 1965 when wheat was no longer grown on the farm.

The south end of the barn is an enclosed corncrib measuring 4 feet by 42 feet. A separate corncrib just to the east of this part of the barn collapsed during a 1987 wind storm.

Ten of John and Catharine's fourteen children were born at the home on the Old Philadelphia Pike. In 1844 John Stoltzfus was ordained to the office of deacon in the Amish church. The next year he and his family moved eight miles east to the Millwood area. John Stoltzfus's position in the church probably influenced his decision to move. He soon became a prominent leader in a progressive movement which had strong support in the Lower Pequea Amish church district, near Millwood. Trouble was brewing in several Amish communities about this same time. Divisions between progressive and conservative factions occurred in several Amish settlements in the 1850s. The progressives, who became known as Amish Mennonites, modified many Amish practices, such as changing from the custom of meeting for worship in homes to the use

(top) At one time the windmill pumped water to this large wooden tank in the north end of the barn. Piped to the house the force of gravity provided pressure without the use of a water pump. Around 1975 when the wooden water tank was no longer water tight, it was retired from use.

(bottom) The spacious barn has ample room for hay storage. Bales of corn fodder are also stored here and used as bedding for the cattle. When the barn burned down on July 4, 1908, a large crop of loose hay filled the mows. The huge volume of smoldering hay delayed cleanup.

of meetinghouses. The Lancaster Amish churches had avoided getting involved in the controversy for many years but a division finally did come to Lancaster County in 1877 when an Amish Mennonite church was organized at Millwood. As a precursor to this event John Stoltzfus moved to Tennessee in 1872 where he helped establish an Amish Mennonite settlement. Among the Lancaster County Amish, he became known as Tennessee John Stoltzfus. He died in 1887 in his new home.

Jacob and Elizabeth Lapp, Staunchly Amish

When John Stoltzfus sold his farm in 1845, he divided it into two plots. Jacob Lapp, the son of John's brother-in-law, Michael Lapp (the first Amish owner of the farm) bought the northern part of the property—72 acres along the Old Philadelphia Pike, including the house and barn.

Jacob Lapp married Elizabeth Beiler in 1840. They had grown up on neighboring farms near Ronks. No doubt a major event during their youth was the 1834 construction of the Columbia-Philadelphia Railroad which passed between their homes. Young Jacob and Elizabeth probably watched with fascination as the railway progressed, marveling at the early horse-drawn rail cars and the later steam locomotives. This particular railroad was one of the first built in the United States.

Both Jacob and Elizabeth were from steadfast Amish families. Elizabeth's father, David Beiler, became an Amish minister in 1822 and a bishop in 1831. Jacob's father, Michael Lapp, was ordained deacon in 1839. Both men were talented writers. Michael Lapp compiled a collection of devotional writings. David Beiler wrote *Das Wahre Christentum*, a lengthy treatise on Amish beliefs. A staunch defender of traditional Amish faith and practice, Beiler's sentiments for the time-honored ways of the past are fervently reflected in his 1862 memoirs.

After Jacob and Elizabeth Lapp moved to the Stoltzfus farm, there were undoubtedly significant changes in the discussions around the dinner table. The liberal ideas of Jacob's uncle, Tennessee John, gave way to the more conservative and traditional Amish views of people like David Beiler and Michael Lapp.

Jacob Lapp's Untimely Death

Jacob and Elizabeth's marriage only lasted fifteen years. Jacob Lapp died on March 28, 1855 at the young age of 36. Sensing his impending death, Jacob wrote his will on Christmas Day 1854, only three months before he passed away. In his opening remarks he stated that he did not know how much longer he would live. He expressed his utmost concern for the spiritual and material welfare of his wife Elizabeth and his three children: Mary age 11, Jacob Jr. age 8, and Elizabeth age 1½.

Jacob Lapp's will revealed an intelligent and thoughtful man with much foresight. Written in fine German script, the will provided for his wife to continue operating the farm as long as she wished to, or until son Jacob Jr.

Estate Inventory of Jacob Lapp, April 28, 1855

Articles bequeathed to widow:

Cow	$42.50
Carriage	40.00
Bee and box	4.00
Household furniture on Kitchen Loft	5.50
Household furniture on Kitchen	17.50
Household furniture on Milk House	2.00
Household furniture on Cellar	6.00
Household furniture on Garret	6.50
Bed, Bedstead and Chairs	4.75
Chest contents of same	1.50
Bed, Bedstead, Cupboard &c	5.00
Bed, Bedstead, Chest & c	9.00
Bed, Bedstead, 2 chairs & c	7.00
Stove and Pipe, Chairs, Tables,	
Corner Cupboard & contents & c	15.00
2 Beds and Bedsteads, Bureaus & c	25.00
Contents of another kitchen	28.00

Articles bequeathed to children:

Three Beds and Bedsteads, 4 Chairs,Bureau, & c	45.50

Other items:

Mare and Colt	140.00
3 Horses	325.00
Colt	50.00
24 Cow and Steer Chains	10.50
Ladder	1.50
Plantation wagon and two sets of boards	57.50
Ladders	10.00
Hand Screw, Standard and Log Chains	7.50
Spreaders	3.50
Dung Hook, Shovels & c	1.50
Large Dung fork, Single tree and other forks	4.50
5 cows	142.50
Bull and Two Calves	47.50
Horse Gears, Halters and Halter Chains,	
Saddle, Bridles & c	42.75
Half Bushel, Kettle, Bags & c	2.12½
2 Ploughs	26.75

2 Cultivators and 2 Tooth Harrows	27.50
Wheel Barrow, Spreadder, Sled & c	7.00
Threshing Machine and Horse Power	67.50
Hay Ladders, Hay Pole & c	5.50
Roller	5.00
Windmill and Cutting Box	14.00
Hay	98.00
One Horse Wagon & its Bed	37.50
Wagon, Bed, Bows & c	100.00
Half Bushel Bag, Carriage, Sleigh, Bolster Rope & c	13.00
Wheat and Corn	86.00
Bran, Chop stuff & c	10.80
Oats in the Bushel	45.00
Shorts & c	7.50
About 33 grain Bags	14.50
Rope, Cask forks & c	4.50
Posts and rails intended to be put up on farm	20.50
Potatoes in the ground	16.50
Oats in the ground	54.00
Wheat in the ground	245.00
Grass	150.00
Half of a Corn Shellar	5.00
7 Hogs	50.00
Posts and Boards	35.00
Bran and Corn	1.00
About 250 new Chestnut Rails	29.00
4 Bee Boxes	10.00
Grindstone	3.50
Wood Saw, Cleaver and other tools	7.50
Work Bench, Shaving Horse, Baskets & c	3.25
Flynets	4.00
Spade, Sine Boxes, Corn Cutters & c	1.50
Grain Cradles	8.50
Saddle	5.00
Smoked Pork and Beef	17.50
Potatoes	12.00
Rope, Pully and Brooms	10.00
2 Bridles	2.00

(top) This stone wall along the western "bank" side of the barn is perhaps the oldest construction on the farm. It probably belonged to the pre-1908 barn and may even date to the 1700s.

(bottom) A team of six mules provides horsepower for field work. Stephen Stoltzfus prefers mules to horses because they use less feed and can endure greater heat.

The present dairy herd at the Stoltzfus farm consists of 32 cows. As the importance of dairying increased in Lancaster County, so did the size of the herds. In the late 1800s and early 1900s no more than three to six cows were common on local farms.

became 21. Elizabeth was given the choice of staying at the home place or of building a new dwelling where the tenant house was located on the northwest corner of the farm. The executors were responsible for giving Elizabeth one cow and a hog or two "if she wishes." She was willed a carriage and the use of a shed which Jacob himself had built. In addition, as long as she remained a widow, she was to receive four percent yearly interest from the sum of $2,000.

Each of the children was willed "a good bed and bedstead" and a cow. The girls were to receive a bureau "when they needed one" and Jacob was to get a desk. During the 19th century, as they still are today, furniture pieces and farm animals were traditional parts of a Lancaster Amish young person's dowry. Jacob Jr. was to receive all his father's clothes and, at age 21, "a good horse, saddle, and bridle." Apparently, young Amish men typically rode horseback at this time rather than driving buggies.

Elizabeth Lapp continued to live on the home farm after her husband's death. The 1860 census indicates that Elizabeth was living with her three children and 23-year-old David Z. Beiler. David was Elizabeth's nephew, her brother John's son, and probably served as her hired man.

The Younger Generation Takes Over The Farm

In 1862 the oldest of the Lapp children, Mary (1843-1922), married Joshua Lapp (1835-1919), a second cousin of Mary's father. Tax records indicate that Joshua and Mary Lapp lived on the Jacob Lapp farm between 1863 and 1865.

Two children were born to Joshua and Mary before they moved further east to the area of Buena Vista in Salisbury Township.

Jacob Jr., the only son, married Elizabeth (Betsy) Lapp in late 1870 or early 1871. They were second cousins. Among the Amish, a marriage between second cousins was and still is a relatively common practice. However, marriage to a first cousin or first cousin once removed is forbidden. Lapp is the sixth most common Lancaster County Amish surname. Six percent of Lancaster County Amish people are Lapps (1991).

When Jacob Jr. came of age in 1868, he purchased the family farm at the appraised value of $16,200.18¼. He had been given this option in his father's will. The farm consisted of "77 acres and three perches containing a two-story log dwelling house with a stone kitchen attachment, a stone wash house, a one-story log tennant house, a large stone and frame Swisser barn, a waggon shed and a corncrib."

This description of the farm buildings corresponds very closely to that given in the 1815 tax records. Most likely, the main buildings, which by 1868 may have been almost a hundred years old, were already on the farm in 1815.

Driving horses (those used with buggies) are usually of the standardbred breed. There are three on the Stoltzfus farm.

A new milk house was built after the second Christian Stoltzfus moved to the farm in 1942 (the small addition to the barn on the left).

According to the current Stoltzfus family, the oldest element of the present-day house was built by Jacob Lapp Jr. There is no indication that any part of the present structure is built of logs, so it is almost certainly not the original house which was still on the farm when Jacob Jr. bought it in 1868. The exact time when Jacob Lapp Jr. built his house is unknown, but we may logically assume it was sometime after his marriage.

Stephen Stoltzfus, the contemporary resident of the farm, remembers seeing the remains of an older structure to the east of the present house. This included an elaborate brick "arch" cellar. Arch cellars with their vaulted ceilings were commonly built beneath houses to provide a cool storage place for fruits and vegetables. Dairy products and baked goods were also often kept there. Occasionally these cellars were dug at separate places rather than underneath the house. It may be that the arch cellar remembered by Stephen Stoltzfus was either part of the original house on the farm or a cellar which at some time had been constructed outside the main dwelling. There was also an old hand-dug well close to this location which was probably the original source of water for the homestead. This well was used into the early 1900s.

In Jacob Lapp Sr.'s will, his widow Elizabeth Lapp was given "a place to live in the big room (*Grosse Stube*) in the place we now live. Which ever one of the downstairs bedrooms (*Kammer*) she wants, and the hall between the two bedrooms, and two upstairs bedrooms, half of the wash house, and half of the garden." These arrangements were made in reference to the old house but a similar arrangement was apparently made after the new house was built. According to tradition, Elizabeth occupied the northern part of the oldest section of the present house. She was said to have had a separate entrance to the house and her own stairway to the second floor. Elizabeth probably lived with this arrangement for about twenty-five years.

Jacob Lapp Jr. Becomes Weavertown Jacob

In 1877, at the age of 31, Jacob divided 14 acres from the northwest corner of the farm and relocated to this plot. This is where the log tenant house had been located, but Jacob probably built a new house. The crossroads to which Jacob and Betsy moved was called Weavertown and from that time he was known as Weavertown Jacob Lapp (*Vayfuh Schteddel Check* in the Pennsylvania German dialect). Since children were and still are important in the day-to-day operations of an Amish farm, Jacob and Betsy Lapp's move to a smaller place may have been influenced by the fact that they had no children.

Jacob Lapp was ordained to the ministry in 1902 at the age of 56. People living today (1991) remember Jacob's sermons. He was especially fond of children, even though he had none of his own, and often geared his messages to the younger generation. He also conducted German language classes for local Amish young people.

A man of wisdom, who was occasionally called to help settle church disputes, Weavertown Jake was a prolific writer of both prose and poetry. He specifically mentioned his books and writings in his will, thus indicating a sizable collection. Evidently, he inherited talent from his two grandfathers, Michael Lapp and David Beiler. Jacob Lapp was also one of the founders of the Amish Aid Society in the 1880s. This organization was the Amish answer to fire insurance.

A particular bit of folklore among local Amish people revolved around Jacob Lapp's hay. As the story goes, it never rained on Weavertown Jake's hay. One year a neighbor asked Jake when he planned to cut his hay. When Jake replied, "Tomorrow," the neighbor thought it was safe to cut his own hay, which he did. Meanwhile, Weavertown Jake was called upon to take care of some church duties and did not cut his hay. It rained on the neighbor's cut hay.

Sometime during Weavertown Jake's sojourn on the Stoltzfus farm an arrangement was made with neighbor Daniel Esh concerning a spring that had been discovered on the Esh property close to the boundary of Jake's land. The spring produced so much water that Esh agreed to share the excess with the Lapps. A terra cotta tile pipeline was put in extending to the Lapp farm. Weavertown Jacob also laid a branch of pipe to his new home. However, because of the lay of the land, the branch never worked too well. From this time on the water rights for the spring were mentioned in all the deeds relating to the Lapp-Stoltzfus farm. While the spring provided an abundance of water for most of the year, it predictably dried up every summer.

The Sojourn of Christian K. Stoltzfus: a Time of Sorrow

The 60 acres of the Lapp farm that contained the old homestead were rented to Eli Renno in 1877. In 1878 Christian K. Stoltzfus moved there from the Leola area.

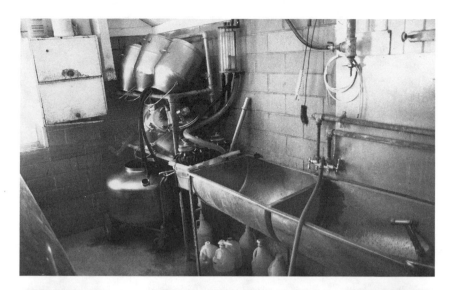

(top) Christian Stoltzfus installed a mechanical milking system soon after he moved to the farm. Operated by a vacuum pump powered by the diesel engine, this system, like those used by other Lancaster Amish, is an older style which uses individual buckets attached to each milking unit. The milk from these buckets is poured into the portable tank (on the floor to the left).

(bottom) In the 1960s milk companies pressured Amish farmers into installing bulk storage tanks for milk. Stephen Stoltzfus put in his first tank in 1964. In 1986 he replaced that tank with the 600-gallon tank pictured in this photo.

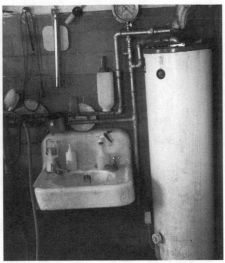

(left) Because milk companies required that milk be agitated periodically, the Amish developed battery-operated agitators triggered by timers.

(right) Stringent sanitation laws necessitate a hot water heater. This one operates on propane gas.

Christian had married Elizabeth Lapp, the youngest of Jacob and Elizabeth Lapp's children, in 1874. Christian and Elizabeth rented the farm from Weavertown Jacob Lapp, Elizabeth's brother, until 1883 when they bought the farm. Elizabeth Stoltzfus had only spent four years of her life away from the place of her birth.

Her mother, widow Elizabeth Lapp, was still living when the Stoltzfuses bought the farm and provision was made for her in the deed. She was given the right to "hold and occupy the four north rooms in the dwelling during her natural life, together with the cellar below and the attic above said room, with free right of way to same or any part thereof. Also the use of that part of the house yard immediately north and west of her portion of the dwelling: also to use water from the well and cistern, and to stable her visitors' horses in the barn."

Christian and Elizabeth had two daughters—Mary and Emma—when they moved to Elizabeth's home place. Seven more children—five daughters and two sons—were born to the Stoltzfuses while they lived at the farm along the Old Road.

Christian, although not a minister, was a well-respected member of the Amish church. He served on the Amish Aid Society for many years.

During their years on the farm, a series of sorrows beset the Christian K. Stoltzfus family. Daughter Emma died at the age of four on January 10, 1882. About five years later another tragic event more directly affected the family of Christian Stoltzfus's second cousin, Jacob Stoltzfus, who lived on a farm across the Old Road and to the north of the Stoltzfus farm.

A Tragic Train Accident

Around noon on October 18, 1887, Nancy Kauffman Stoltzfus and Barbara Kanagy Stoltzfus drove down the long lane of the Jacob Stoltzfus farm in a horse-drawn carriage. They were on their way to a corn-husking frolic at the home of Jonathan King. Barbara was visiting from Kansas. Her husband, Isaac Stoltzfus, was a first cousin to Nancy's husband, Jacob Stoltzfus.

At a railroad crossing just east of Ronks their wagon was struck by a train. The vehicle was demolished and the horse was dragged 75 to 100 yards down the track. Nancy was killed instantly and Barbara lived only a few minutes. The bodies were taken to the nearby porch of the Jonathan Smoker home and later moved to Nancy's home.

The funeral was held at the Jacob Stoltzfus farm. According to a newspaper story, "Vehicles of every description, Amish wagons, carriages, buggies, and open wagons lined the fences all about the premises, and by actual count there were two hundred and seventy vehicles on the spot, in addition to at least fifty at the neighboring farm of Christian Stoltzfus."

The Death Angel's Frequent Visits

In a relatively short span death visited the Christian Stoltzfus family several times. Daughter Mary died in 1894 at age 19. Although the circumstances are unknown, the records show she died of lockjaw after a four-day illness. According to family tradition, Mary's boyfriend, who lived at a distance, did not find out about her death until after the funeral. In 1896 daughter Rebecca died at age 15 after suffering from paralysis for six months. The elderly grandmother, widow Elizabeth Lapp, passed away at the age of 79 on October 16, 1896. A widow for 41 years, Elizabeth never remarried after the untimely death of her husband, Jacob Lapp Sr.

Perhaps most tragic of all was the death of Elizabeth Lapp Stoltzfus, age 43, on March 11, 1897. She had been ill with pneumonia for one week. Christian K. Stoltzfus was left behind with six children, including an infant son slightly over a month old. Around a year later in 1898, forty-six-year-old Christian Stoltzfus married twenty-five-year-old Lovina Fisher. One child, Sadie, was born to this union in 1899. After only nine years of marriage to Lovina, Christian died in 1907 at the age of 56. He had been in poor health for the previous six months. Four of the Stoltzfus children were still living at home. Lovina moved to a house along Weavertown Road which Christian had purchased in 1894, and rented to various people until his death. Lovina Fisher Stoltzfus married Daniel Esh in 1911. She died at age 45.

Two Brothers Continue Farming

In Lancaster County most Amish marriages take place in the month of November. Following this custom, Jacob L. Stoltzfus, oldest son of Christian K. Stoltzfus, married Susan King on November 27, 1906. They were both twenty years old.

As most Amish couples do, they spent the next few months visiting friends

The use of propane gas and compressed air are two rather recent concessions which the Amish community has made to the modern world in order to stay in the dairy business.

and relatives. Not until the next spring did they set up housekeeping. On April 7, 1907 as Jacob and Susan were getting settled on the home farm, Jacob's father died. Instead of sharing the responsibilty of the farm with his father, young Jacob suddenly became the head of the household. For reasons which are not entirely clear, the ownership of the farm reverted to Weavertown Jacob Lapp after the death of his brother-in-law, Christian Stoltzfus. Jacob and Susan Stoltzfus, with the help of Jacob's younger brother Elam, continued to farm what had been their father's farm.

Barn Fire

A year and several months after the death of Christian Stoltzfus, the farm suffered another loss. On July 4, 1908 the huge bank barn was completely destroyed in a fire. The July 11, 1908 *New Holland Clarion* gave the following report:

COUNTY SWEPT BY HEAVY ELECTRICAL STORM
The rain came down in torrents in many sections last Saturday afternoon. Considerable damage done.
Christian L. Stoltzfus, living at Molasses Hill in East Lampeter Township, is the loser of between five and six thousand dollars as the result of lightning striking the barn. The building was burned to the ground together with implements and this season's hay and wheat crops. The livestock was all saved.

There are three errors in the newspaper report. First, the farm is in Leacock not East Lampeter Township, although it is very close to the border. Second, Christian K. Stoltzfus was mistakenly given the middle initial L. Furthermore, Christan was no longer living at the time of the fire.

The Stoltzfus farm is, in fact, located near Molasses Hill. According to local legend, a horse-drawn cart carrying a barrel of molasses had leaked out a large quantity of the gooey substance as it climbed the hill many years earlier.

Elam Stoltzfus, who was interviewed in 1990 at age 94, remembered the fire quite vividly. Eleven years old at the time, he lived with his newly-married brother Jacob and wife Susan.

According to Elam Stoltzfus, the morning was spent putting wheat shocks into the barn. The barn also was filled with hay from that summer's abundant crop. The storm came in the afternoon, and lightning probably struck the windmill mounted on top of the barn. The windmill was used to power a corn sheller and feed grinder.

The fire spread very quickly. Much effort was made to prevent the house from burning, keeping the roof of the summer kitchen soaked with water. Fortunately, the cows were not tied in the stable and escaped easily. The cattle ran down the road and various neighbors caught them and provided care for them. Once the structure had burned down, the hay and straw smoldered for a week, hindering the clean up process.

A large barn raising typical of later years did not happen at the Stoltzfus farm in 1908. A dozen or so workers showed up every day until the barn was

This diesel engine performs many functions on the Stoltzfus farm. It powers the mechanical milkers and the bulk tank's cooling mechanism. The engine also operates an air compressor (for the lighting system in the chicken house and for the water purifier) and a hydraulic pump (to pump water).

The building on the right was built by Jacob Stoltzfus in the 1930s as an implement shed. It still serves as a shelter for farm machinery, but it also contains the farm power plant—the diesel engine. Note the air and hydraulic lines extending from the shed. Exhaust from the engine provides pressure to pump manure from an underground tank up the spout seen on the left of the building. In the foreground stands a manure spreader.

completed. The first job was to reconstruct the wall around the base of the barn. The stone wall along the bank side of the barn on the west had survived. Today, it is probably the oldest piece of construction on the farm.

The large beams for the barn were made from logs floated down the Susquehanna River and sawed at the river town of Marietta. Transported to Ronks by rail, the wood was picked up with horse-drawn wagons and carried to the Stoltzfus farm.

Farming in the Early 1900s

According to Elam Stoltzfus, Amish farming practices have changed considerably since the early 1900s. Over a four-year period, most Amish farmers practiced a four-crop rotation. A hay crop was followed by corn. The next year the field was planted with a combination of tobacco and potatoes followed by wheat. After the wheat the field went back to tobacco and potatoes for one year followed by hay, after which the cycle began again. When Elam lived on the farm, there was an orchard south of the barn. In the 1883 deed Jacob Lapp reserved the fruit of seven apple trees for ten years. There is no sign of this orchard today.

Plows were the walk-behind type, not the riding kind used by most Amish farmers today. Hay was raked with a dump rake rather than the more modern side-delivery rake. Put into small piles to dry, it was manually loaded onto hay

This cement block building was built as a carriage house and stable in 1970 for Christian Stoltzfus. It is now used by Stephen Stoltzfus.

wagons with two-pronged forks. Today it is most often baled.

Corn was cut by hand and placed in shocks. Husking was done in the field from the shocks. Tobacco was planted by hand rather than with mechanized planters. Watering the tobacco plants was a back-breaking job which no one enjoyed.

Wheat shocks were stored in layers in the barn, awaiting a threshing machine. The crop was threshed over time, rather than all in one day. Elam Stoltzfus remembered both portable gasoline engines and steam engines being used to power threshing machines. He knew of some farms that had special sheds for horse powers (a power unit propelled by horses traveling in a circle), but none were used at the Stoltzfus farm during his time.

In the early 1900s tax records show there were six or seven cattle over four years old on the Stoltzfus farm. From 1911 to 1913 ten cattle were listed. According to Elam Stoltzfus, twelve cows were considered a large herd at this time. Three or four horses were shown for the farm during this period, and from 1911 to 1915 one dog. Cream was sent to an ice cream plant in Lancaster. Milk was put in 100-pound cans and taken to Ronks where it was picked up by a train and shipped to Philadelphia.

The Line is Broken

In 1915 twenty-nine-year-old Jacob Stoltzfus, his wife, five children and eighteen-year-old brother Elam moved to the White Horse area in Salisbury Township. Two of Jacob's sisters had married and moved to this area earlier which may be part of the reason he chose to relocate there.

Weavertown Jacob Lapp sold the old home place to John B. Petersheim.

Before selling, he took ten additional acres from the farm and added it to his own place near Weavertown. The Stoltzfus farm became the 52-acre farm which it still is today.

For the first time in 90 years, the farm on the Old Road passed out of the hands of the Michael Lapp family. John Petersheim and his wife Rebecca (Smucker) had only two sons. John had been ordained a minister in 1914, the year before they moved to the farm on the Pike.

The main contribution John Petersheim made to the farm was an improved water system. A galvanized pipe was laid to replace the old terra cotta tile to the spring located on the property of Amos Kauffman (formerly Daniel Esh). The pipe installed by Petersheim directed the water to a steel trough on the back porch of the house. From there, the water flowed to the milk house where it served to cool milk cans. Finally, the water went to the barn where it was used by the livestock.

Jakey and Fannie: A Unique Amish Couple

John Petersheim sold the farm to Jacob K. Stoltzfus in 1921 and moved to a place a short distance to the east along the same road. Jacob K. Stoltzfus had married in 1919 at age 32 to Fannie Ebersol who was seven years his senior. Born to Amos and Katie Stoltzfus on the farm just across the Old Road, Jacob was not quite a year old when his grandmother, Nancy Kauffman Stoltzfus, was killed in the train accident near the Ronks crossing. Jacob's grandfather, also Jacob Stoltzfus (the third in a line of Jacob Stoltzfuses), remarried to widow Rebecca Lantz Lapp, the mother of the folk artist and furniture maker, Henry Lapp. Fannie was a niece to Barbara Ebersol, the dwarf Amish folk artist whose decorative fraktur book plates became prime collector's items in the 1980s.

Jacob (called Jakey) and his wife Fannie were a very unique Amish couple. Jakey and his brother Jonathan (called Yonie) were deaf. The Stoltzfus brothers received a special education at a school for the deaf in Philadelphia. As a result, they learned to lip read and speak rather effectively in English, but could not communicate in the dialect of the Amish, Pennsylvania German. Other Amish people marveled at how they could talk to each other and never make a sound. Jonathan, who never married, shared farming responsibilites with his brother Jacob on their adjoining farms.

For an Amish man, Jacob developed several unusual interests. He learned to operate a sewing machine at the school in Philadelphia and made his own clothing. In later years he made quilt tops.

He also carried on the regular operation of the farm, usually without any particular handicap. For example, when he was working in the fields, he knew when Fannie rang the dinner bell by the way the horses responded to the sound.

Since she had no children, Fannie involved the neighborhood boys in her chicken operation. The chickens were free-roaming and often laid their eggs in odd places. Fannie gave a few cents to the boys for each egg they found. Little did she know that some of the smaller boys were crawling through the hole used

This windmill was probably constructed by Jacob Stoltzfus in the 1920s to pump water from a new well which supplemented the property's original hand-dug well. The small structure at the base of the tower once served as a milk house where milk cans were cooled with flowing water. When the wind is not strong enough to turn the wheel at the top of the windmill, a hydraulic pumping system powered by the diesel engine is used. Many Amish farms in Lancaster County no longer use windmills or water wheels to pump water.

With the coming of indoor plumbing the outhouse became obsolete and was discarded.

(top) On a rise to the south of the Stoltzfus farm a windmill stands on the edge of a large orchard. In the late 1800s owner Daniel Esh noticed a patch of damp ground and decided to dig a well. This spring of water proved more than ample for the Esh farm. The excess water was allowed to flow to the Stoltzfus farm.

(bottom) During certain times of the year, water from the spring is abundant. To conserve some of this water Stephen Stoltzfus built a 12' x 30' underground cistern. Despite the abundance of water, it does not last all year. The spring predicatably goes dry during the summer. Water from the well near the house is pumped to this cistern to allow for a gravity flow system.

by the chickens to gain access to their house and gathering eggs directly from the nests.

During the 1920s and 1930s Jakey and Fannie made many improvements to the farm and its buildings. A wash house or "kettle house," so called because of the large iron kettles mounted in a brick stove which served to heat water and perform large cooking tasks, was built. It had an outhouse on one end and a smokehouse for curing meat on the other end. They put up an implement shed east of the barn and a concrete silo on the south side. Between the house and barn, they built a chicken house which sheltered about 100 fowl. Jakey may also have built the small milk house with a windmill in the area near the chicken house. They dug a new well, put in a cistern behind the barn for watering livestock, put asphalt shingle-type siding over the old, dark green, wooden "German" siding on the house and installed a new sill under the whole house. A tree in the yard, which is now a large, shady maple, was planted by Fannie during their stay on the farm.

In 1932 a certain notorious guest spent some time in Jakey's barn. A fierce bull had taken the life of Jacob K. Petersheim on his farm north of Intercourse. As the story goes, when the undertaker brought Jacob Petersheim's body back to his home where the funeral would be held, the bull began bellowing uncontrollably. Jakey Stoltzfus offered to take the wild animal to his barn since he had an extra sturdy stall made of steel pipes. The bull stayed at the Stoltzfus farm for six weeks before being sold to an artificial breeder. The animal was considered too valuable to be destroyed.

The *Freundschaft* Returns

Jacob and Fannie Stoltzfus decided to rent out their farm when they were in their sixties. Of the fifteen people who wanted the farm, Jakey chose Christian K. Stoltzfus (1907-1983) primarily because he was a grandson of the former owner of the farm by the same name. (He was born the same year the first Christian K. died.) Christian, his wife Emma (Beiler) and four children moved from near White Horse in Salisbury Township onto the farm in 1942. Thus, the farm returned to the Lapp–Stoltzfus *Freundschaft* (family line) after twenty-seven years. Christian K. and Emma Beiler Stoltzfus bought the farm in 1949. The youngest of the Stoltzfus family was born at the farm several years after they moved there. Jakey and Fanny Stoltzfus moved to a house a short distance to the west on the north side of the Old Road.

The Stoltzfuses made a number of changes soon after they came to the farm. Christian had a herd of about 16 cows, average for that period, but an addition to the barn was necessary to accommodate them. He also built a new milk house with a water cooling trough. Later when Grade A milk buyers required the use of mechanical coolers, Christian installed one. A type of hoist helped to lift the heavy milk cans in and out of the cooling trough and the cooling tank. For a while both methods for cooling milk were used.

Around this time, Christian Stoltzfus also installed a mechanical milking system. A diesel engine in a small shed beside the milk house powered the vacuum pump for the milking system and the refrigeration unit for the mechanical cooler. All of these innovations were within the boundaries of the *Ordnung* (rules and regulations) of the Lancaster County Old Order Amish.

More cows meant more milk but also more manure. Before this time, a shovel and wheelbarrow had been sufficient to haul the waste matter away. Christian Stoltzfus put a litter carrier into the barn to help move the extra volume of natural fertilizer. As this large steel container was pushed through the stables on a steel track, manure was shoveled into the bucket and dumped into a manure spreader parked at the end of the barn.

Growing Tobacco

Like many Lancaster County farmers, Christian Stoltzfus grew tobacco. During his years on the farm, he usually planted about five or six acres of tobacco each year.

Tobacco crops require long hours of toil and tender loving care. In fact, the intensive labor involved in growing tobacco endears the crop to the Amish community. Amish parents welcome the year-round work of tobacco growing because it keeps their children occupied. A commonly heard adage among the Amish is, "Idleness is the Devil's workshop." In the case of tobacco the malevolent nature of the crop is overlooked for the wholesome work it provides, although a growing movement in the Amish community questions the wisdom of this practice. Each year fewer Amish farmers grow tobacco.

Soon after the second Christian Stoltzfus moved onto the farm in 1942 this 600-hen chicken house was built. It replaced a smaller chicken house built by Jacob Stoltzfus which sheltered about 200 hens. The first structure was torn down about 1972.

The tobacco season starts in March when the local tobacco steamer takes his steam traction engine from farm to farm, steaming the tobacco beds to kill the weed seeds in the soil. Along with the tobacco seed, radish seeds are sewn in the beds which are covered with hog bristles and sheets of muslin. Since the radishes are hardier, they grow faster and push the muslin away from the fragile, maturing tobacco plants. The beds are watered frequently and after about three weeks the muslin is removed and the radishes are picked. (They are said to have a better flavor because of the frequent watering.)

By the last part of May the tobacco plants are ready for transplanting. The beds are watered down thoroughly and the plants are carefully removed and placed in compartments in a transplanter. A team of horses or mules draws the transplanter through the fields. The machine requires a driver and two people who remove the plants and insert them into the soil at regular intervals. The transplanter automatically waters each plant.

While the plants grow, they require a lot of cultivation. The two-horse cultivator used on the Stoltzfus farm had special "hoers" which cultivated between the plants with a lever-operated arm.

In addition, tobacco fields require tedious hand hoeing each season. Later, when the stalks are larger, they must be "topped"—a process which involves breaking off the bud of the main stalk. This promotes growth in the leaves. Small shoots or "suckers" begin growing where the tops have been broken off. Until recently these had to be removed by hand but now a special spray inhibits the growth of suckers.

In mid-August the tobacco crop is ready to be harvested. The stalks are cut at the bottom with long handled shears. They are then speared onto long sticks called laths with a removable metal point. The tobacco laden laths are placed on a special wagon and taken to the barn. Many Lancaster County farms have separate tobacco barns used for drying the tobacco. Since the regular barn was quite large, the Stoltzfus farm never had a separate tobacco barn.

By late November the tobacco has dried, and the laths filled with tobacco stalks are moved from the drying barns to a damp cellar. On the Stoltzfus farm this was an earthen-floor underground room beneath the western projection of the barn.

After the dried tobacco stalks have moistened, the leaves are stripped from the stalk. Stripping the tobacco leaves provides work for most of the winter.On the Stoltzfus farm, as on most Amish farms, there was a special stripping room in the southern end of the barn.

Sharing the Load

In the days before and immediately after World War II, Amish farmers commonly shared equipment and labor. Christian Stoltzfus went together with an unrelated neighbor and a brother-in-law. The three families helped each other with harvesting their various crops—hay, corn, potatoes and tobacco. They also shared some pieces of equipment. Threshing and silo filling especially became important social events, thus making the toil more enjoyable.

The egg business was greatly expanded when this three-story, 6,000-layer house was built in 1959. It featured a slatted floor which allowed for easier manure removal. Chickens no longer occupy this building. Its first floor has been used for heifer pens.

Right after World War II the Stoltzfuses obtained a corn binder. This machine cut the corn stalks near ground level and tied them into bundles which were loaded onto an accompanying wagon. The arduous task of cutting corn stalks by hand before feeding them into the silage cutter was thus eliminated.

Christian also bought a hay baler in the late 1940s; he was one of the first Amish farmers to do so. This machine, although pulled by horses, used an engine to power the mechanism. In addition to baling his own hay, Christian was hired to bale hay for neighboring farmers. A few years later a hay conditioner or hay crusher was purchased. This machine crushed the hay so it would dry more evenly.

The Rise and Fall of the Potato

In the 1940s and 1950s many Lancaster County farmers grew potatoes as a cash crop. Christian Stoltzfus shared a potato planter, motorized potato digger and a potato grader with the two other farmers in his circle. In the early 1950s Christian designed a flail chopper or rotabeater for use in potato fields. When driven through the fields in the fall after the potato vines had died, this motorized device chopped up the weeds and the old potato vines, making it easier to dig the potatoes. Christian did custom work for other farmers with his chopper.

During harvesting time neighborhood boys were hired to load baskets of potatoes onto wagons. Potato buyers came around to individual farms and the farmers sold their crop immediately after harvest if the price was good. Otherwise they stored the potatoes in the barn, waiting for a better price. Most Amish farmers stopped growing potatoes when large mechanized operations pushed the small growers out of the market. Christian Stoltzfus grew potatoes until 1957.

With several sources of income gone, Lancaster Amish farmers increasingly concentrated on dairy farming. The Stoltzfuses found that chickens were also economically feasible.

An Expanding Chicken Operation

In the 1940s Christian Stoltzfus had built a second chicken house, which held 600 chickens, near the location of the original log dwelling and just east of the current house. The old chicken house Jakey and Fannie had built was then used as a buggy and tool shed and was finally torn down about 1972. In 1959 a three-story chicken house was built southeast of the barn. This one could handle 6,000 chickens. The 1940s chicken house was used for a while to raise chicks, but like the Jakey Stoltzfus chicken house also eventually became a buggy shed and shop.

Changes to the House

Christian and Emma Stoltzfus decided that the wash house would be more convenient if it were closer to the house. Fannie Stoltzfus had insisted that it not be attached to the house to lessen the danger of the house catching fire. The wash house which Jakey Stoltzfus built was carefully taken down and moved piece by piece. Its smokehouse and outhouse appendages were not rebuilt.

In the 1950s a number of household innovations were accepted by the Amish, including indoor bathrooms. Modern plumbing was possible with gravity flow systems that do not require electric pumps. At the Stoltzfus farm water from a spring was piped to the house and barn, using the gravity flow system. When this was not sufficent, a windmill or gasoline engine pumped water to a large tank elevated in the barn. From here the water was piped to where it was needed.

The 1950s also introduced the widespread use of propane gas for cooking, heating water and refrigeration to the Lancaster Amish. The Stoltzfus farm was no exception. Before this time, cooking had been done on a range that burned either coal or wood. There was also an auxiliary kerosene burning stove. Refrigeration was provided by an ice box. Ice was delivered to the farm periodically.

The house was heated with coal burning stoves, but in the 1950s kerosene burning heaters were introduced to the home. These were fed from large outside storage tanks.

The Present Owner

Christian's oldest son, Stephen, married Nancy Blank in 1958. The couple set up housekeeping on the Stoltzfus farm. In 1959 they built an addition to the west side of the house for Christian and Emma in typical *Dawdy Haus* Amish fashion. A separate small barn was built for Christian's horse and buggy in 1970.

Christian continued to manage the chicken operation until 1967 when ill health prevented him from continuing. In 1970 the farm was turned over to son Stephen.

The chicken business expanded even more in 1975 when a 280-foot-long chicken house was constructed. This house holds 12,000 caged layers.

Like an increasing number of Lancaster Amish farmers, Stephen Stoltzfus stopped growing tobacco. The last tobacco crop on the Stoltzfus farm was harvested in 1960. The dampening cellar was sealed off, and the stripping room was remodeled into additional stable space.

Like many Lancaster farmers the Stoltzfuses also stopped growing wheat because they could no longer compete with the huge wheat farms in the West. Stephen Stoltzfus had his last wheat crop in 1965. Some local Amish farmers still grow a little wheat, primarily for the straw because the grain is worth comparatively little. Threshing frolics, once a festive occasion on Lancaster Amish farms, are consequently rare in today's Amish community.

Christian Stoltzfus had always used horses for draft work on the farm but Stephen switched to mules. He determined that these hybrid animals gave more work and could take more heat for less feed. Like most mules used by Lancaster Amish farmers, the Stoltzfus mules are not raised locally. The current team comes from Florida.

The last major piece of farm equipment to be introduced to the Stoltzfus farm was a corn picker which was purchased about 1967. Like other pieces of equipment designed to be pulled by tractors, the corn picker was equipped with an engine which powered the picking mechanism. The equipment itself was pulled through the fields with mules.

Lots of Layers

Stephen continued to expand the chicken business. In 1975 a 280-foot-long, 12,000 cage house was built southwest of the barn. When this new house and the 1959 house were at peak operation, there were 18,000 birds on the farm. Later, the three-story 1959 house was phased out and the first floor was used for heifer pens. The other floors were not used.

It is a well known fact that chickens lay more eggs when there are more hours of daylight. Modern farmers easily extend the amount of light with electric lights and electric timers.

The Stoltzfus chicken house uses a system invented by an Amishman named Ben Fisher, utilizing standard Coleman-type lanterns attached to an air line. The lanterns must be lit individually, but they stay lighted through a system of compressed air regulated by a battery-operated timer. When the air is cut off, the lights go out.

In contrast to many modern egg operations in the county, all the feeding and egg collecting in the Stoltzfus chicken house is done by hand. The eggs are gathered once a day and stored in a refrigerated room until the buyer picks them up.

While the Stoltzfus chicken operation is large compared to earlier years, it is quite small compared to the mammoth chicken farms elsewhere in the county. The business which currently buys the eggs from the Stoltzfus farm prefers eggs from smaller farms because such farms generally have more variety in egg size (the older the chicken the larger the egg). Large chicken operations generally move chickens in and out all at one time which means all of their chickens are usually about the same age. Formerly, several local restaurants bought most of the Stoltzfus eggs. Stephen and Nancy Stoltzfus also sold eggs to local people directly from their home from 1969 until 1986.

Unlike the many large chicken operations in Lancaster County, the design of the Stoltzfus chicken house requires collecting the eggs and feeding the chickens by hand.

(top) After the eggs are collected, they are stored in a cool room at the front of the chicken house.

(bottom) The pressurized mantle lanterns which light the chicken house must be individually lit, but a battery-controlled timer switches off their air supply at a specified time, thus turning them off.

Change and Expansion in the Dairy

When Stephen Stoltzfus took over the dairy herd in 1959, there were 14 cows. He gradually added to the herd, which, for a while, meant milking in more than one shift because the cow stable had only 16 stalls. By 1987 there were 32 cows.

In the 1960s the milk companies who bought from Amish farms insisted that milk be stored in stainless steel bulk storage tanks rather than the traditional milk cans. One of these bulk tanks holding 400 gallons was installed on the Stoltzfus farm in 1964.

To provide for the increased dairy herd, the Stoltzfuses constructed a bunk feeder in 1969 and added a 14'x 60' silo in 1972. This same year the diesel engine was moved to the old implement shed to the east of the barn primarily to decrease the noise level. The barn itself was renovated in 1970, replacing the stone and wood foundation wall around the lower perimeter of the barn with cement block. In 1986 a new 600-gallon bulk milk tank replaced the 400-gallon tank.

In 1988 a new method for storing silage was tried. A large white plastic bag, called an "Ag Bag," was placed on the ground and blown full of ensilage. The end result looked like a gigantic caterpillar.

New Methods for Manure

In the 1970s the litter carrier installed by the first Christian K. Stoltzfus was replaced. The new system utilized a horse-drawn, blade-like device pulled through the manure gutters. It scraped the manure out one end of the barn into a manure spreader.

Stephen's younger brother, Christian, invented a unique manure handling system installed at the Stoltzfus farm in 1986. The new method involved pushing the liquid manure into a 20,000 gallon underground holding tank. Exhaust from the diesel engine used to power the milking equipment was piped into the tank, exerting pressure on a movable plate which compressed the manure. When manure was needed to fertilize fields, a spreader was parked under a large spout connected to the manure tank. By moving a lever a flow of manure was released into the spreader.

Christian Stoltzfus got the idea for his invention after observing a road emergency crew using exhaust from a truck to inflate a large bag which was used to upright an overturned truck trailer.

In 1991 there were plans to install a manure composting system at the Stoltzfus farm. This ecologically aware method involves mixing the liquid manure with dry material, such as saw dust or dry chicken manure, in order to bring it to a temperature at which bacterial action is most beneficial. The manure is placed on a long narrow stockpile by means of a conveyor belt.

Water and Power

Currently (1991) the farm power plant serves a variety of purposes. In addition to its original jobs of powering the vacuum pump for the milking system and the refrigeration unit for the bulk milk tank, the diesel engine now also powers a cooling unit for the egg storage room, a generator to recharge batteries for buggy lights, a hydraulic motor which runs a water pump designed to augment the pumping power of the windmill and an air compressor which runs both a separate pneumatic water pump for a water purifying system and the pressure lighting system in the chicken house.

Water from the well is pumped to a large cistern at the top of the southern slope on the farm. This 20,000-gallon concrete tank constructed in 1978 also serves as a reservoir for the spring which lies a little higher on the slope. Also in 1978 a new plastic pipe replaced the galvanized pipe from the cistern. Water from the cistern flows to the farmstead by force of gravity because the cistern is at a higher elevation than the farm buildings. An old wooden tank in the barn originally installed for gravity flow has not been used for water storage for several years.

From Generation to Generation

Christian K. Stoltzfus died in 1983 at the age of 76. His funeral was held in the barn at the home farm. Widow Emma continued living in the *Dawdy* side of the house until 1987 when Stephen's newly married son Daniel and his wife Anna Mary moved onto the farm. Stephen and Nancy and the youngest son, Reuben, moved to the *Dawdy* side of the house. Grandmother Emma moved to the home of one of her daughters. Stephen's two oldest sons had married and moved to farms in the far southern end of the county. The third son located in the eastern part of the county. In 1990 Reuben married and set up housekeeping at another location along the Old Road. He continued working at the farm equipment manufacturing shop of his uncle.

Daniel and Anna Mary Stoltzfus officially bought the dairy herd soon after moving onto the farm in 1987. Thus, as is typical among the Amish, Stephen Stoltzfus went into semi-retirement at age 49. However, he has not been idle. A sixth generation descendant of Michael Lapp, the first Amish owner of the farm, Stephen still owns the farm and does his full share of the farm work. He is also active with his brother in experimentation and installation of manure composting systems. In addition, Stephen is a member of the local Amish historical group and takes part in land preservation efforts. Nancy keeps busy quilting for a local shop and frequently babysits for her grandchildren.

Non-Amish Owners and Residents

1. 1761   William Hamilton (c.1720-1781)
Jane (McMasters) (c.1719-1808)
   From Belfast, Ireland and settled in Lancaster County
   sometime before 1745.

2. 1761   John Woods (? -1770)
Jane and/or Mary

3. 1766   George Woods (1740-1776)
Mary
Son of John and Jane Woods

4. 1778   John Henry
Mary

5. 1795   Peter Miller (1746-1815)
Mary (1739-1825)
   Came from York County, Pennsylvania. May have
   been a Mennonite.

6. 1802   Daniel Miller (1772-1824)
Barbara (Stoner?) (c.1775-1853)
Son of Peter Miller

Amish Owners and Residents

7. 1825   Michael Lapp (1796-1855) md. 1817
Barbara (Stoltzfus) (1801-1890)
   Bought the land but apparently never resided on
   the farm.

8. 1827   John Stoltzfus (1805-1887) md. 1826
Catharine (Hooley) (1807-1884)
   Brother to Barbara Stoltzfus Lapp

9. 1845   Jacob Lapp (1818-1855) md. 1840
Elizabeth (Beiler) (1817-1896)
   Son of Michael Lapp

10. 1862   Joshua Lapp (1835-1919) md. 1862
Mary (Lapp) (1843-1922)
   Daughter of Jacob and Elizabeth Lapp

11. 1866   Jacob Lapp Jr. (1846-1923) md. 1870
            Elizabeth (Lapp) (1852-1912)
                Son of Jacob and Elizabeth Lapp

12. 1878   Christian K. Stoltzfus (1851-1907) md. 1874
            Elizabeth (Lapp) (1853-1897)
            Lovina (Fisher) (1872-1917) md. 1898
                Elizabeth was the daughter of Jacob and Elizabeth Lapp

13. 1906   Jacob L.Stoltzfus (1886-1949) md. 1906
            Susan (King) (1886-1939)
                Son of Christian and Elizabeth Stoltzfus

14. 1915   John B. Petersheim (1873-1947) md. 1898
            Rebecca (Smucker) (1870-1956)

15. 1921   Jacob K. Stoltzfus (1886-1972) md. 1919
            Fannie (Ebersol) (1879-1970)

16. 1942   Christian K. Stoltzfus (1907-1983) md. 1928
            Emma (Beiler) (1909-)
                Grandson of Christian and Elizabeth Stoltzfus

17. 1958   Stephen E. Stoltzfus (1938-) md. 1958
            Nancy (Blank) (1936-)
                Son of Christian and Emma Stoltzfus

18. 1986   Daniel J. Stoltzfus (1964-) md. 1986
            Anna Mary (Lantz) (1965-)
                Son of Stephen and Nancy Stoltzfus

5.
The Holmes County, Ohio, Amish Community

The rolling hills of Holmes County, Ohio, are home to the largest Amish settlement in the world. Farmsteads such as this one near the village of Charm, date back to the first half of the 19th century. Note the large barn, the large farm house and the smaller Dawdy Haus.

In 1808 Bishop Jacob Miller and his two sons made the 200-hundred mile trek from Somerset County, Pennsylvania, to the Sugarcreek Valley in Ohio. They claimed a tract of land and built a cabin. This was the beginning of what would become the largest Amish community in the world. The Millers originally settled in Tuscarawas County. Beginning in 1809 the majority of Amish moving from Somerset County to Ohio established themselves a few miles to the west in Holmes County. Eventually the Amish would also expand into

In Holmes County most Amish houses have white siding. Porch extensions on the front and back of the house are typical. While the barn on this farm is white, red barns are considered more traditional among the Holmes County Amish.

Wayne County to the north and into Coshocton County to the south, but the settlement has usually been known as the Holmes County settlement.

In addition to being the largest Amish community in the world today, Holmes County also holds the record for the largest number of Old Order Amish groups. In 1992 there were nine distinct fellowships of Amish people in the area. All of these groups use horse-drawn vehicles and have German language church services in their homes. Differences between the groups center around various fine points of doctrine and technology. There are also at least fifteen more modern groups which descend from the first Amish church in the Holmes County area but today identify themselves as Mennonites or Amish Mennonites.

In 1900 there were seven Old Order Amish districts in the Holmes County settlement. By 1925 it had doubled to fourteen, by 1950 it had more than tripled to forty and by 1975 it had doubled again to eighty-four. In 1992 there were 145 Amish church districts in the heavily populated Amish community around Holmes County, Ohio. This number includes some church districts which are called New Order Amish.

(top) The main part of the barn on this farm has a gambrel roof, a recent innovation among the Amish. The large shop building to the right of the barn illustrates that even the very rural Holmes County Amish are establishing non-agricultural businesses on their farmsteads. Note also the gas well, a welcome source of energy on many Holmes County Amish farms.

(bottom) In Holmes County the main farmhouse usually is not attached to the Dawdy Haus as illustrated in this photo. The form of the smaller house on the right is quite characteristic of Amish houses in Holmes County.

(top) Holmes County Amish farms average over a hundred acres, often twice the size of a typical Lancaster County Amish farm. However, since much of the land in Holmes County is quite hilly, the two communities average much closer in tillable acres per farm. Note evidence of strip mining in the background of this well kept Holmes County farm.

(bottom) Smaller than most Holmes County Amish houses, this dwelling is typical of pre-Civil War buildings. Its two stories, white siding, front and back porch extensions and walk-in, daylight basement are all characteristics of traditional Holmes County Amish houses.

(top) Amish farms often include a great variety of buildings, many of which have several additions. In front of the traditional large farmhouse stands a house trailer, possibly used as a Dawdy Haus.

(bottom)Many newer Amish houses in Holmes County are still quite plain and simple. Note the unusual arrangement of windows, indicating the focus on interior usefulness rather than outward symmetry.

Despite the presence of large brick factories in nearby Sugarcreek, few Holmes County Amish houses are built of brick. The architecture of this home is quite atypical, illustrating an innovative trend among younger Amish families.

6.
The Yoder–Miller Farm of Holmes County, Ohio

This farm was the pioneer homestead of the Schlabach family in Holmes County, Ohio. Christian and Jacob Schlabach moved here in 1826. Three generations now dwell in the house complex, the youngest being the eighth generation to live on the farm.

The Hills of Holmes

The rolling hills of eastern Holmes County, Ohio, and its four neighboring counties are home to the largest Amish community in the world. In some areas one can drive for miles on gravel roads, see nothing but Amish farms and meet more buggies than cars. In many of the small villages Pennsylvania German is more commonly heard than English.

The first Amish settlers in Holmes County came from Somerset County, Pennsylvania, in 1808 and many more followed over the next several decades. According to folklore, there are seven hills on each farm in Holmes County while in the more mountainous Somerset County, there are seven farms on each hill. Many people from the Amish settlement in Somerset exchanged one

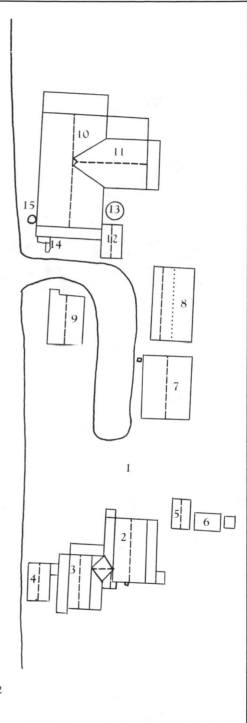

1. Site of old spring house
2. Main house
3. *Dawdy Haus*
4. Woodshed
5. Wash house
6. Chicken house
7. Grinding shed
8. Buggy shed
9. Repair shop - 1965
10. Barn - ca. 1840
11. Staw shed - 1943
12. Hog house - 1964
13. Silo
14. Milk house - remodeled 1972
15. Feed bin

(top) In typical Holmes County style the houses on the Yoder-Miller farm have enclosed front and back porches. Unlike many local Amish homes, the main house and the Dawdy Haus are connected.

(bottom) The farm's large poplar tree sprouted from a walking stick owned by Joas Schlabach. After his death, it was discovered in the spring house and transplanted to its current site. The building behind the tree in this photo was once a woodshed. Since wood is no longer burned for heat, it serves as a storage shed.

(top) *The large bank barn on the Yoder-Miller farm is thought to have been built by Jacob Schlabach in the 1840s.*

(bottom) *The original structure of the barn has been added to several times. The extension to the right was built as a straw shed in 1943. The white hog house in the foreground was added in 1964.*

The hay on the Yoder--Miller farm is now baled. Until 1958 it was piled loose in the mows using ropes and grapple hooks.

kind of hilly terrain for another in the early 1800s. One such Amish family was that of the patriarch Christian Schlabach who moved from Somerset to Holmes in 1826.

The Schlabachs Come to America

In 1819 the Schlabach family lived near Jesburg in Hesse, Germany, on what was known as the Richenroth estate. Because civil law did not permit Amish people to own land, the Schlabachs probably rented or leased from some noble or prince. Like many other Amish people in Europe after the Napoleonic Wars, the Schlabachs looked to the New World for a better life.

In March of 1819 John Schlabach, age 36, along with Christian Schlabach Jr., age 25, set off for America to scout out the land. Perhaps they also hoped to find marriage partners since they, like all four of the Schlabach brothers, were single. After disembarking in New York, John and Christian Jr. made their way west across the Allegheny Mountains to the Casselman River Valley in Somerset County, Pennsylvania. There were three different Amish settlements in Somerset County at that time. The first Amish to settle in the area came as early as the 1760s from Berks County, Pennsylvania, and neighboring areas of southeastern Pennsylvania.

According to tradition, the Schlabach brothers were divided in their feelings about the desirability of the new land. Evidently, John was not favorably impressed, but Christian Jr. felt differently. Without John's knowledge, Christian sent word for his parents to proceed to America. The elder Christian Schlabach and his family arrived in Baltimore on September 30, 1820, eight days after Christian's sixty-ninth birthday. As the story goes, John and Christian Jr. were working in a field when they saw a man approaching in the distance. Christian thought the man looked and walked like their father but was puzzled by the strange hat he was wearing. As the man drew nearer both young men realized it was indeed their father, Christian Schlabach. One can especially imagine John's astonishment. As it turned out, the hat was purchased in Baltimore because Christian's traditional Amish hat had been lost at sea.

Although the Schlabachs probably lived in Somerset County for six years, there is no record of any of them ever owning land. Apparently they only rented. While Somerset did not prove to be the land of promise in this respect, three of the Schlabach brothers did find wives in their new home. In fact, the women Jacob and Daniel Schlabach married supposedly influenced the Schlabach family's decision to move to Ohio.

It is said that Henry Yoder, a wealthy Amishman in Somerset County, offered three quarter sections of land (480 acres), which he owned in Holmes County, Ohio, to the men who would marry his two single daughters. While this sounds like a folktale, it is a fact that Jacob and Daniel Schlabach married Barbara and Catherine Yoder, the daughters of Henry Yoder. The two couples occupied land in Ohio which Henry Yoder had purchased. One of these quarter sections was deeded to Henry Yoder by President James Monroe in 1818. The location of the land was given as "northwest of the Ohio and above the mouth of the Kentucky River."

The marks of the broad axe are still visible on the massive beams in the barn. Wooden pegs hold the structure together.

Straw is blown into the straw shed part of the barn using a "wind stacker" on the threshing machine.

A New Home in Ohio

In 1826 most of the Christian Schlabach family moved to Holmes County, Ohio. In addition to Jacob and Daniel and their wives, this included Christian and Magdalena Schlabach who were 75 and 66, respectively, the oldest son John, who never married, and the youngest daughter Anna, who also remained single. A daughter Magdalena married Jacob Kempf only a short time before or soon after the move to Ohio. The oldest daughter Mary and her husband Daniel Eash also made the move west. In 1831 Catherine, the daughter who had stayed behind in Germany with her husband John Gingerich, also moved to Holmes County.

Probably the last of the Schlabachs to move to Holmes County was Christian Jr. Perhaps he was reluctant to leave because it was on his urging that the family came to Somerset. It is not known exactly when Christian Jr. relocated. In 1832 he and his family were still in Somerset County. However, according to records, Christian Jr. died in Holmes County in 1871. His wife died in 1868.

Occupying the Land

Jacob and Daniel Schlabach evenly divided the 480 acres of land deeded to them by their father-in-law Henry Yoder. The grandparents Christian and Magdalena resided on the farm of their oldest married son Jacob. It is probable that a separate house was built for the grandparents since they lived for more than another decade. Christian died in 1840, and Magdalena in 1843. They were the first to be buried in the small family cemetery on the Yoder-Miller

(top) A large beam running the whole length of the barn is visible in the cow stable. Three generations of the Yoder-Miller family usually help milk the 15 cows by hand each morning and evening.

(bottom) Milk from stainless steel buckets (on the left) is poured through a strainer into old-fashioned milk cans (on the right).

farm. In 1991 new gravestones were put in place to mark the burial of these two Amish pioneers. Before this time simple fieldstones located the graves of Christian and Magdalena Schlabach—the one marked merely C S, the other uninscribed. This well kept cemetery was once in the woods, but now lies in the middle of an open field.

It is thought that Jacob and Barbara Schlabach built a small, simple house, no doubt of logs, for their first dwelling place. Family tradition maintains they originally had only a blanket for a door which kept Barbara awake at night fearing that wolves might enter their abode. Jacob and Barbara had two small daughters when they moved to Ohio and the following year twins were born. In 1834 they had their last and seventh child.

Jacob Schlabach probably built a second house when the original log cabin became inadequate for his family. With a basement constructed of sandstone, this second structure was insulated with poured mud and is thought to be the oldest part of the present-day house. Mud was obtained from a nearby mudhole and stirred with a horse-powered device. This type of construction was a variation of European-style half timbering or *Fachwerk*. Several other houses in Holmes County have been discoverd which were built this way. Such structures are not easily detected because they were covered with wooden siding thus concealing the distinctive features.

A spring house which once stood very close to the site of the original cabin may have served as a dwelling for a time. The spring house was torn down when the foundation became unstable, but, even then, the solid frame of the structure resisted demolition. An outdoor bake oven which once stood near the house also was torn down years ago.

The barn on the farm is thought to date to the 1840s. The great stone foundation wall, the broad axe marks on the timbers and the unusual length of some of the floor beams seem to verify the age of the structure.

The Family Grows

The 1850 census shows that Jacob and Barbara Schlabach (spelled Slaubaugh in the records) lived together with their children Catherine, age 26, Elizabeth, age 22, Jacob, age 20 and Susanna, age 16. Living in the same dwelling house but listed as a separate family were David Schlabach, age 21 and his wife Catherine, age 18. Whether the two families actually lived under the same roof or in separate but adjacent houses is not known. It is thought that David built what is now the *Dawdy* (grandfather) part of the house complex.

The census records for 1860 reveal that David and Catherine Schlabach (this time spelled Schlaughbaugh) had five small children. Living close by in another house were Jacob Schlabach, age 74, John Schlabach, age 78 and Catharine Schlabach, age 36. It appears that Jacob's bachelor brother came to live with him in his old age and that Jacob's oldest daughter, who was not yet married, cared for the two elderly men. Jacob's wife had died in 1856. This arrangement changed sometime in 1860 when Catherine married widower John Schmucker. Jacob died in 1863 and John probably died sometime before 1870.

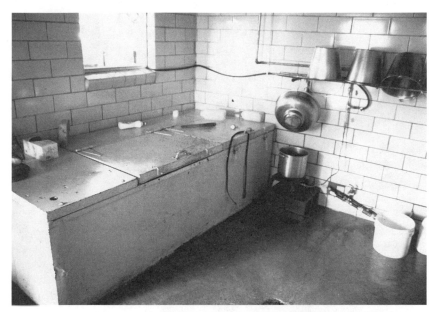

(top) *Full milk cans are placed in this concrete water tank for cooling. In 1989 a mechanical cooling unit was added to maintain the lower temperatures required by the milk buyer.*

(bottom) *The full milk cans are picked up every morning by a truck from the cheese house. In earlier years each farmer hauled his milk by horse-drawn wagon to the cheese house.*

About a hundred pigs are kept on the Yoder-Miller farm.

A Prominent Resident

Sometime after David Schlabach's parents passed away, his father-in-law came to live with the family. This was none other than Levi (*Leff*) Miller, a prominent figure in Holmes County Amish history. Levi had been one of the key conservative leaders in the Old Order Amish-Mennonite division in the 1860s. In fact, the Old Order Amish church in Holmes County was sometimes called *Die Leffy Gma* (The Levi Church) in Levi Miller's honor. The progressive Amish church was called *Die Mosey Gma* (The Moses Church) after *Gross* (Big) Mose Miller, a second cousin of Levi's who was married to Levi's sister Catherine.

Levi Miller had been involved in the dispute between the progressive and conservative factions among the Amish from the beginning. In 1851 he traveled to Mifflin County, Pennsylvania, to help settle a controversy about the mode of baptism. (The progressives wished to baptize people as they knelt in a stream.) This was the first issue that arose to divide the two factions.

As the two camps moved further and further apart, some leaders called for a national meeting of Amish ordained men. An unusual step for the highly congregational Amish, the first meeting in 1862 was dominated by the progressive group. Levi Miller was among those who voiced objection to the lack of representation for the conservatives. The progressives wished to mediate compromises between the two groups, but the conservatives felt that compromise would result in departure from the true faith. At the later 1865 Amish conference Levi Miller became the spokesman for the conservatives. A paper was presented which listed the points the conservatives would not yield on. The progressive group seems to have ignored the conservatives and a permanent rift

(top) From left to right are a hay rake, a grain binder, a hay baler (covered with canvas) and a hay tedder. The baler is attached to a "fore cart" which makes it possible to pull tractor-designed equipment with horses.

(bottom) This ground driven hay mower is used to cut hay in the field. The cut hay is then tedded, raked and baled.

(top) The corn binder (left) cuts corn stalks and ties them in bundles. The corn bundles are brought to the barn and fed into a silage cutter (right) which chops up the corn and blows it into the silo using a long tube.

(bottom) Even among the Amish, old-fashioned grain binders are becoming a rarity. Fewer small farmers are growing wheat and binders like this one used on the Yoder-Miller farm have not been produced for nearly fifty years.

(top) *This old-style manure spreader on the Yoder-Miller farm was originally designed to be pulled by horses. Tractor-type spreaders attached to a fore cart are also common among the Amish.*

(bottom) *Nine farmers belong to the threshing ring which shares this threshing machine. It is driven from farm to farm during wheat and oat harvest.*

This Case tractor provides power to drive belts during threshing and silo filling. It is not used for field work. Rubber tread bolted to the steel wheels protects the road surface when the tractor is driven from farm to farm.

resulted. The progressive Amish group eventually lost all Amish distinctives and merged with the Mennonite Church.

Levi Miller served as a leader in the Amish church for many years, but as his age advanced he became senile and required more and more care. When he no longer had his faculties, he was confined to a room in the David Schlabach home. A granite-top table still exists which bears scars made by Levi's fork. Levi died in 1884 at the age of 85. He is buried in the cemetery on the Yoder-Miller farm beside his daughter, Catherine Schlabach, who helped care for him during his last years. His wife is buried a few miles away.

Joas Schlabach, a Handicapped Artist

David Schlabach divided his land among three of his children before he died in 1895. Joas Schlabach, the ninth of David's ten children, became the owner of the current Yoder-Miller farm. Joas married Catherine Troyer in 1893. For a number of years there were two Catherine Schlabachs living on the farm. Both were known as Katie. In typical Holmes County fashion they were differentiated by their husbands' first names. The older woman was called David Katie and the younger woman was called Joas Katie. In 1906 David Katie died quite suddenly. Joas Katie found her with her apron full of cracked corn ready to feed the chickens.

Joas suffered from poor health due to heart problems for most of his life. His hair turned white at a young age. Perhaps because of his physical disabilities, Joas developed some artistic talents. Several examples of his multi-colored fraktur work have been preserved. One such piece featured an illustrated list of businesses in the village of Charm in the early 1900s. Pencil drawings by Joas Schlabach adorned the interior walls of the barn at the Yoder farm for many years. He died in 1914 at the age of 43.

A remarkable memorial to Joas survives on the Yoder farm to this day. He evidently left a walking stick in the spring house. It sprouted and was planted. Today it is a beautiful, large poplar tree.

Rudy Yoder, a Faithful Soldier of the Cross

Joas Katie was left with four children between the ages of ten and twenty-one. The oldest child, Elizabeth, married Rudy Yoder on December 21, 1919 and the farm once again prospered.

While his marriage occurred late in 1919, the early months of that same year also marked an eventful time in the life of Rudy Yoder. As a twenty-three-year-old youth Rudy had been drafted into military service on October 3, 1918. During World War I the United States government made no provisions for conscientious objectors. Young men from the peace churches (Amish, Mennonite, Brethren, Quaker) were forced into Army camps. After registering Rudy was sent on a train to Camp Jefferson, Missouri. On arrival he told the registrar he was a conscientious objector. Rudy was the only person in the large assemblage of men to take such a stand. After taking part in one marching drill, he realized he could not participate in any more.

This glazed block building was the original home of Jonas Yoder's harness shop. After the business moved to its new quarters near son Leroy's home, the block building once again became the farm repair shop.

107

Much pressure was exerted to wear an Army uniform, but Rudy consistently refused. One day while he was taking a shower, his clothes were taken from him and replaced with a uniform. He wore the military garb for over a week until Rudy's father and another Amish man from Ohio appeared in camp with his Amish clothes which had been sent home. The young man stepped out in faith and put his Amish clothes back on. This act was met with boos from his campmates. Two days later two officers led Rudy to a hill near the barracks. He was shown three freshly dug graves and was told that boys who had refused to wear uniforms were interred there. Rudy was given one day to put the uniform back on or he would be in a fourth grave. He calmly told the officers that his mind would not change and stated simply that the teachings of Jesus forbad participation in war. Despite lots of angry shouting, cursing, waving of guns and physical shaking, Rudy endured. When the officers realized their efforts were in vain, they marched Rudy back to the barracks. For three weeks Rudy was subjected to ridicule and abuse by the soldiers, but he endured through prayer and reading the Bible.

On November 9 he was suddenly transferred to Camp Sherman in Ohio. (Another source says Camp Taylor, Ohio.) While Camp Sherman had about 100 conscientious objectors, they represented only a small minority among the thousands of soldiers stationed at the camp. When the war ended soon after Rudy's arrival at Camp Sherman, he was detained four more weeks. He served as assistant cook for the camp. On January 6, 1919 his thirteen-week ordeal finally came to an end.

Despite many hardships and physical infirmities, Rudy J. Yoder was known as a cheerful, outgoing person and a gifted storyteller among the Holmes County Amish. He suffered from a serious back injury caused by a fall from a cherry tree. Also when he was around forty years old, he was attacked by a stray cow and left with several broken ribs. Even after he had to have an eye removed, he maintained his cheery personality.

As the story goes Rudy was once waiting at a feed mill when a young prankster came up from behind and hit him on the side of the head. Wanting to teach the boy a lesson, Rudy groaned, held his head and quickly took out his glass eye which, with feigned agony, he showed the boy. The young man certainly never tried that trick again.

To the farm itself Rudy Yoder made one important addition. He built a chicken house on the opposite side of the road from the house. All the water for the birds was hand pumped at the house and carried across the road. Since the approximately 400 birds produced enough eggs to pay for all the animal feed on the farm for many years, this extra effort was considered well worth the trouble. Rudy sold the eggs in the village of Charm, driving there by horse and wagon.

Rudy Yoder spent the last seven years of his life almost totally blind. One of his grandsons remembers how he would hold him up to the light of a window in order to see at least an outline of his form. Rudy died in 1968 at the age of 74.

Since 1981 there has been a natural gas well on the Yoder-Miller farm. Like most Amish farmers in Holmes County, the Yoders and Millers use natural gas for heating and cooking.

The Farm Is Strip Mined

Rudy and Elizabeth Yoder had five children—four girls and one boy. The only son, Jonas R. Yoder, married in 1954 and set up housekeeping on the home farm. He officially bought the farm in 1958.

Jonas soon piped water to the chicken house across the road. By this time an egg buyer picked up the eggs at the farm. When the egg market declined, Jonas Yoder felt the chicken business was no longer worthwhile. In the late 1960s the poultry operation at the Yoder-Miller farm ended. A few chickens were kept around the farm for domestic use.

Several major changes have come to the farm in the last twenty years. In 1972 Jonas was approached concerning the possibility of strip mining his land for coal. Although he was quite reluctant at first, he finally conceded. A stipulation in the contract stated that no excavating could be done within one hundred feet of the family cemetery. The first step involved drilling narrow holes at various places on the farm to find the coal. Once the location was established, a fleet of bulldozers and earthmovers moved in and began working on the west side of the road. A one-foot layer of top soil was removed and put on a pile. The next layer of two or three feet of subsoil was then put on another pile. The big machines dug an average of thirty feet in search of the black substance. In addition, a lot of fire clay—the raw material which supports the thriving brick factories in nearby Sugarcreek—was also found.

The mining companies were required by law to restore the land as nearly as possible to the way it was. Immediately after extracting the coal, the restoration work began. Actually, they even made a few improvements. A high bank on the west side of the road was removed and several deep gullies were filled in. Better drainage was provided which eliminated the need for drainage tiles. The road was straightened and a steep hill was flattened. The entire process took two years—one year for the west side of the road and one year for the east side.

The government also required the strip miners to make sure the land produced as well as it had before the disturbance. At the Yoder-Miller farm, it did even better at times. Some of this fertility was created when large quantities of lime were added to the soil. The one detrimental effect of the strip mining was much looser soil which no longer held moisture as well during a dry spell.

During the mining a windmill-pumped well, which had been contaminated by sulphur, was destroyed. The restoration process produced a deeper and better well on the hill north of the house. Today a windmill pumps water into a large holding cistern. The water then flows by force of gravity to the house. The old Rudy Yoder chicken house, unused for several years, was also torn down during the mining.

More Buried Treasure

Less than ten years after the farm was mined for coal, a request to extract another treasure from beneath the soil came. In 1981 a natural gas well was dug in the field across from the house. An abundant source of petroleum for several years, it gradually declined. Although the sale of gas decreased, the Yoders still use gas from the well free of charge.

Most Amish viewed the presence of natural gas on their properties as a gift from God, and it was not considered wrong to make use of it. The acceptance of this new fuel brought many technological changes which would normally happen much more slowly in an Amish community. On the Yoder-Miller farm gas replaced wood and coal for cooking, heating and water heating. Gas was even piped into the hog house and milk house for heating.

Non-Modern Milking

When Jonas Yoder was a boy, the animals on the farm included eight cows, a couple of hogs and a few chickens. Today the farm has fifteen cows, about twenty-five heifers, a hundred pigs and some chickens.

The cows are still milked by hand. Most Old Order Amish in Holmes County have avoided the bulk storage tanks and mechanical refrigeration equipment required for Grade A milk by selling their milk to cheese companies. Until 1989 the milk on the Yoder-Miller farm had been cooled in milk cans with natural flowing water. When the local cheese company insisted on lower temperatures for the milk, a mechanical cooler was installed on the Yoder–Miller farm. However, the milk is still stored in the metal milk cans which are then placed in the chilled water.

In the days of Rudy Yoder four or five milk cans were hauled to the village of Charm in an open wagon called a "milk hack" every morning. As many as twenty wagons lined up at the cheese house waiting to deliver their milk. The farmers did not regard this waiting time with impatience but welcomed it as a time to visit and catch up on community news. After the milk was poured out, the cans were filled with whey (a milk by-product) which the farmers fed to their pigs. In the early 1950s the cheese house began sending a truck around to the farms to collect the milk. The cheese plants stopped giving whey to the farmers because they could send it to a whey products plant in Sugarcreek.

Other Changes on the Yoder–Miller Farm

Sometime around 1948 indoor plumbing was installed in the Yoder house. Before this an outhouse served as the bathroom. A pitcher pump on the porch was used to pump water from a twenty-foot hand dug well directly beneath the porch. Water was carried into the house.

Like many Holmes County Amish families, the Yoders make use of a sort of natural air conditioning. Every summer the family traditionally moves its kitchen and living room quarters to the spacious and well-lighted basement. Many Holmes County Amish houses are built into the sides of hills and have basements with ground floor entrances and windows on one or more sides.

A team of large Belgian work horses provides the main source of power on the farm. With the exception of a hay baler, the farm implements are all of the traditional non-motorized type. Until 1958 hay had been gathered loose with

The Yoder farm was strip mined in 1972 and 1973. In the process the old well was destroyed. A new well was drilled on the rise south of the house. A windmill pumps water into a large cistern from which it flows by force of gravity to the house. In the background is son Leroy's house and the harness shop where Jonas and Leroy work.

The small family cemetery on the farm was in a wooded area when the first graves were placed here in the 1840s. Five generations of the Schlabach family are buried here.

an old-style hay loader. Jonas Yoder says his father Rudy remembered the time when hay loaders themselves were innovations. In those days the hay was raked by hand and stacked loose in the barn using ropes and grapple hooks. In many barns the grapple hooks could be moved along the length of the barn with a "hay car" which ran on a track. There was no such track in the Yoder barn, and the hay had to be carefully and quickly swung by rope to where it belonged. Guiding the horse which pulled the rope and triggering the jaws of the hooks so they let go at just the right second required a considerable amount of skill.

Most of the farm equipment used on the Yoder-Miller farm today is owned by the family. However, a very old (as all such implements now are) Hart threshing machine is shared by nine area farmers. A tractor nearly as old as the thresher powers the machine. During wheat and oat harvest, the threshing operation moves from farm to farm. The tractor also powers a silo filler (ensilage cutter). Never used for field work, the tractor has steel wheels covered with rubber tread.

A much enjoyed social event comes at the end of the harvest season. All the families involved in the threshing ring gather at one of the farms. The purpose of the meeting is to settle financial matters related to the use of the threshing equipment. However, the fringe benefits include a time of fun and fellowship with roasted hot dogs, homemade ice cream and volleyball.

A New Business

About 1978 Jonas Yoder bought a heavy duty sewing machine and began making nylon halters for horses. He eventually expanded into making and repairing harnesses and experimented with a nylon harness which at first proved unsatisfactory. Later Jonas discovered a special kind of plastic-coated nylon material called "Biothane" which worked well for harnesses. It was actually stronger than leather and much easier to clean.

Jonas Yoder's nylon harnesses for both buggy and draft horses became quite popular in the Amish community and even among non-Amish horsemen. The business grew beyond the glazed block building which had originally been constructed as a farm repair shop in 1965. In 1989 Jonas and his son Leroy, who had joined him in the business, decided to build a large sheet metal structure near Leroy's new home several hundred yards from the Yoder-Miller farm.

The Yoder–Miller Farm's Current Occupants

At the age of 43 Jonas Yoder was chosen by lot to serve as a minister in his local Amish congregation. He felt a need to be relieved from some of the farm responsibilities.

In 1976 Jonas Yoder's daughter Arlene married Roy Miller. Roy gradually took over the farm work and eventually bought the farm in 1991. Roy and Arlene Miller's four children are the eighth generation of the Christian Schlabach family to live on this farm.

Residents of the Ohio Farm

1. 1826　Jacob Schlabach (1786-1863) married ca. 1824
   Barbara Yoder (1793-1856)
   　　　Born in Germany, moved to Somerset County,
   　　　Pennsylvania in 1820 and to Holmes County, Ohio in 1826
2. 1850　David J. Schlabach (1828-1895) married ca. 1850
   Catherine Miller (1831-1906)
   　　　Son of Jacob and Barbara Schlabach
3. 1893　Joas D. Schlabach (1871-1914)
   Catherine Troyer (1873-1950)
   　　　Son of David and Catherine Schlabach
4. 1919　Rudy J. Yoder (1894-1968)
   Elizabeth Schlabach (1893-1977)
   　　　Daughter of Joas and Catherine Schlabach
5. 1954　Jonas R. Yoder (1929-)
   Anna R. Yoder (1929-)
   　　　Son of Rudy and Elizabeth Yoder
6. 1976　Roy L. Miller (1955-)
   Arlene J. Yoder (1956-)
   　　　Daughter of Jonas and Anna Yoder

7.

The Elkhart–LaGrange, Indiana, Amish Community

The flat expanses of northern Indiana are the home of the third largest Amish community.

The Amish community which occupies the eastern part of Elkhart County and the western part of LaGrange County in northern Indiana is the third largest Old Order Amish settlement in the world. Like Holmes County, Ohio, the first Amish to come to this area emigrated from Somerset County, Pennsylvania. In 1841 two Miller brothers and two Bontrager brothers started west from the northernmost of the three Somerset Amish communities. This settlement actually extended into Cambria County and was known as the Johnstown settlement. In the 1840s and 1850s many other Amish families from this area relocated to Indiana, eventually rendering the Johnstown settlement extinct.

A number of families from Holmes County, Ohio, also moved to Elkhart and LaGrange Counties in the early years. Although these Holmes County people were descendants of Amish people who had moved from Somerset to Ohio thirty years earlier, there were various differences in practice between the Holmes County people and those who moved directly from Somerset County to northern Indiana. In 1854 the majority of those with Holmes County background divided from the northern Indiana Old Order Amish and formed progressive Amish Mennonite churches. There is a neighboring Amish settlement in the vicinity of Nappanee, Indiana. This community actually started earlier than the Elkhart-LaGrange settlement (1839) but has always been the smaller of the two (20 districts in 1992).

In the Elkhart-LaGrange Amish community all of the church districts fellowship with each other in spite of significant differences from one district to another in what technological advances are acceptable. This is especially true regarding farm equipment. For example, some church districts still forbid the use of hay balers, while other neighboring districts allow their members to use hay balers. The Elkhart-LaGrange community also fellowships with the Nappanee community.

In 1900 there were five Old Order Amish church districts in the Elkhart-LaGrange settlement. By 1925 the number had doubled to ten, by 1950 it more than doubled to twenty-five districts and by 1975 it had almost doubled again to forty-six. In 1992 there were 78 Old Order Amish church districts in the thriving Elkhart-LaGrange Amish community of northern Indiana.

This house and barn are quite large by Indiana standards. A Dawdy Haus addition appears to be attached to the main part of the house, creating a "T" formation.

Simple white houses and small barns are the general rule on most Elkhart-LaGrange Amish farms like those pictured on pages 116-117.

117

(top) A high percentage of Amish barns in the Elkhart-LaGrange community have gambrel (hip) roofs.

(bottom) In some parts of the northern Indiana Amish Community one sees what may be described as an Amish suburbia, with many small barns and houses lining the rural roads, most of which are occupied by Amish families. More than half of the heads of Amish families in northern Indiana work in factories. Several acres, a small barn to shelter a horse and buggy and a substantial house are home for many of these Amish families. Note the two separate rural Amish homes in this photo.

118

This basic style, sometimes called a "cornbelt cube," was popular in the larger society early in the 20th century. Indiana Amish builders continue to construct houses with these characteristic pyramidal hip roofs.

Newer Amish houses in the Elkhart-LaGrange settlement are often starkly simple. Like houses in many Amish communities, they illustrate the emphasis on interior usefulness rather than outward symmetry regarding the placement of windows. The omnipresent enclosed porches are especially useful when church services are held in the homes.

The vehicle in front of this house is a bench wagon used to transport benches for Amish church services. Even families with very small houses, like this one, hold church services in the basements of their homes.

8.

The Bontrager–Miller Farm of LaGrange County, Indiana

Lame John Bontrager moved to the area of LaGrange County, Indiana, known as New Pennsylvania in 1862. He and his family occupied a house built by Jacob Mell about a decade earlier.

Northern Indiana, like much of the state, is a vast flatland of cultivated fields broken only by a scattering of lakes, a grid work of gravel roads and an occasional small town. In one such area just south of the Michigan state line a large Amish community straddles the borders of two counties—Elkhart and LaGrange. In 1991 there were 78 Amish church districts in this Amish settlement, making it the third largest Amish community in the world.

In the Elkhart-LaGrange, Indiana, vicinity many Amish people have the names Miller and Yoder which are also common surnames in Holmes County, Ohio. The third most common Amish surname in northern Indiana is Bon-

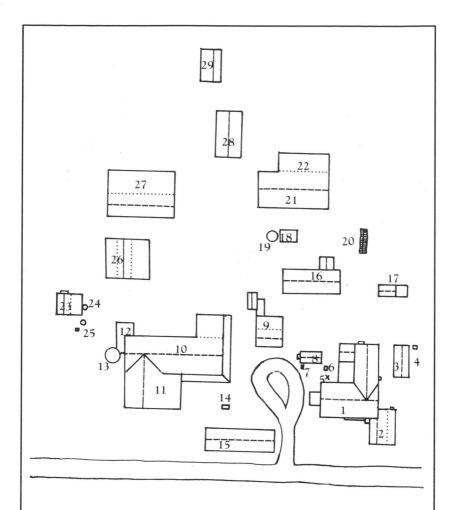

1. Main house - 1873
2. *Dawdy Haus* - ca. 1884
3. Old shop - 1958
4. Outhouse
5. Windmill
6. Well - 1967
7. Dog house
8. Milk house - 1977
9. Buggy shed and storage sheds - early 1900s
10. Main part of barn - ca. 1850
11. Straw shed - ca. 1912
12. Hog shed - 1978
13. Silo - 1930s
14. Watering trough - 1940
15. Hog house - 1990

16. Chicken house - 1934
17. Old chicken house (unused)
18. Old brooder house (unused)
19. Old corncrib (unused)
20. Woodpile
21. Grinding shed - 1967
22. Woodworking shop - 1968
23. Ice house - 1940s
24. Calf shed - 1960s
25. Calf feeders
26. Sheep barn - ca 1890s (addition 1975)
27. Machinery shed - ca. 1929 (addition 1955)
28. Corncrib - 1987
29. Sorghum shed - 1987

The original house burned down in 1873. The house was immediately rebuilt and, through the years, has had various additions. The Dawdy *side of the house (on the right) was probably built about 1884 when Lame John turned the farm over to his son Daniel.*

trager, which is seldom found in Holmes County. There are few Amish Millers and Yoders and no Bontragers in Lancaster County, Pennsylvania. One of the earliest Bontragers to settle in northern Indiana was John Bontrager IV.

The Bontrager Pilgrimage

As a nine-year-old boy in 1844, John Bontrager IV traveled in a covered wagon from Somerset County, Pennsylvania, to Indiana with his parents—John Bontrager III and Anna Bontrager—and their six other children. John III (known as Hans) was ordained to the ministry in the Amish church near Johnstown, Pennsylvania, about 1839. This once-thriving Amish settlement on the border between Somerset and Cambria Counties was one of three Amish communities in the area. The Bontragers had lived in Somerset County, Pennsylvania, from 1767 when Johann Martin Bontrager moved there directly from Europe. It is said that Martin Bontrager and his sons started the first flour mill in the Meyersdale area, which is the southernmost of the three Amish communities.

Martin's son John (John I) moved to the northernmost of the communities at Johnstown. In fact, John Bontrager II (1781-1856) married Barbara Johns (originally Schantz), the daughter of Joseph Johns, who was the founder of Johnstown. Johnstown is the only major North American city named for an

The large barn on the Bontrager-Miller farm was built by the farm's first resident, Jacob Mell, in the 1850s. In 1908 the barn was changed to a bank barn when Daniel Bontrager and a hired contractor jacked up the whole structure, added a concrete wall around the bottom and sloped earth up to the second floor in the back. A silo was built in the 1930s. Various additions have been made to the barn over the yea but the oldest part still has a wood shingle roof.

Hay is brought to the barn loose, fed into an ensilage-style cutter and blown into the mows.

Long ladders are sometimes necessary to extend to the upper reaches of the barn.

Amishman. (Joseph Johns had originally named the town Conemaugh.)

The John (Hans) Bontrager III family was not alone in its move to Indiana. Evidently, there was something of a mass exodus from the Johnstown settlement to Indiana, beginning in the 1840s. Hans' two brothers, Joseph and Christian Bontrager, were among the first Amish families to move to Elkhart and LaGrange Counties in 1841. Eventually all nine of the Bontrager siblings relocated to Indiana, along with father John II himself who made the move at age 67 in 1848.

Settling in Indiana

Upon his arrival in northern Indiana, Hans Bontrager (John III) purchased 160 acres of land for $1550 in Eden Township, LaGrange County from Thomas Hutchinson, the first white man to occupy the land. Much of the land was still wooded. Having received several clockworks as payment for a debt, Hans chose several choice cherry trees from the farm to build cases for grandfather clocks. One of the clocks is still used by descendants of the Bontragers who live at the pioneer homestead (not the farm of this study).

In 1846 the eighth child was born into the Hans Bontrager family and was named for her mother, Anna. Only two years later mother Anna died at the age of 39. Hans married a second time to Mattie Miller from Holmes County, Ohio, and two more children were born to the Bontrager family.

Lame John Bontrager

Adding to the grief of losing his mother, young John IV was afflicted with rheumatism as a teenager. One of his hips was drawn out of joint and the leg did not grow for a period of time, leaving one leg an inch and a half shorter than the other. There was serious concern whether John would ever walk again.

A traveling Indian doctor gave him some herb medicine. He promised to return and told John he expected to see him behind a plow. In less than a year the Indian did return and was delighted to find John back to normal and working on the farm. Of course, with one leg shorter than the other John walked with a decided limp which gave him the nickname "Lame John" for the rest of his life.

Lame John's handicap did not deter him from marrying at a relatively young age. The exact marriage date for John Bontrager IV and Fanny Kauffman is not known, but they must have been younger than 20 since both of them were born in 1834 and their first child was born in 1854. For the first several years of their marriage John and Fanny lived near the Bontrager pioneer homestead in Eden Township.

Brother Joe and the Progressives

In 1854, the year John and Fanny's first child was born, the Elkhart-LaGrange Amish settlement was jolted by a church division. As was the case in many other Amish communities in the mid-1800s, the progressives and conservatives had serious disagreements and parted company. Lame John's father, minister John

Stalls for the Belgian work horses take up a large part of the first floor of the barn.

(Hans) Bontrager, and his uncle, deacon Joseph (Sep) Bontrager, sided with the conservative group which would later be known as the Old Order Amish.

However, Joseph J. Bontrager, an older brother of Lame John's, joined the progressives and in 1867 was ordained to the ministry in the Forks Amish Mennonite church. About ten years later, Joseph Bontrager apparently thought the Forks church was carrying the movement too far. In 1876 he and a number of others withdrew to form the Townline Church which eventually affiliated with the Conservative Amish Mennonite Conference.

When his wife died, Joseph Bontrager soon remarried to his eighteen-year-old housekeeper. Joseph was 51 at the time of his second marriage. A year later in 1883 they moved to Lyon County, Kansas, when neighborhood gossip and informal criticism related to the marriage continued. Later they also moved to Virginia, Illinois and Montana. Joseph eventually reunited with the Old Order Amish and died at age 91, outliving his second wife by nine years.

Moving to New Pennsylvania

In 1862 Joseph Bontrager's brother, Lame John, moved his family nine miles north of the Bontrager pioneer homestead to an area called New Pennsylvania. John and Fanny bought a 143-acre farm, the current Bontrager-Miller farm and the farm of this study, from Jacob Mell (Mehl). The Mells were one of three original families to settle the area, having moved from Pennsylvania around 1850. Each of these non-Amish farmers ultimately moved away when Amish settlers bought the land, but the name New Pennsylvania endured.

Many small items necessary for horse farming and the maintenance of the farm find a niche somewhere in the barn. (See also photos on page 131.)

Lame John bought a few other tracts of land, including 80 acres to the west of his main farm. The 80-acre spread had a thriving huckleberry marsh which attracted pickers from miles around. Thus Lame John was also known as "Huckleberry John." The marsh was eventually drained causing the huckleberries to disappear. Several natural lakes near the Bontrager farm provided an abundance of pickerel, pike and bass. In those days the Bontragers did a lot of spear fishing.

Tragedy Strikes

Adversity first struck the John and Fanny Bontrager farm in 1873 when their house burned down due to a faulty chimney. Five-year-old Manasses Bontrager darted into the flames to rescue a small trunk containing some of his toys and other belongings. Miraculously, he escaped without harm. A new house was soon built with wooden planks and covered with stucco.

Three years later 12-year-old John Bontrager V was struck by lightning and killed while he was inside the barn. Other members of the family were outside in the barnyard milking the cows and were unharmed. A sad time for Lame John and Fanny Bontrager, the death of this son brought a tragic end to the line of John Bontragers.

The Bontrager barn was struck by lightning two more times, but for some reason the building never did catch fire. The second time a bolt of lightning again pierced the barn, killing a young colt. The third occurrence left a team of horses deaf for a time. In keeping with Amish practices the Bontragers chose

(top) A bantam hen finds a secluded spot for a nest in the inner recesses of the barn.

(bottom) The herd of Holstein cows is milked by hand on the Bontrager-Miller farm, but with a large family to help this does not pose a problem.

not to install lightning rods because they believed to do so would be interfering with the work of God.

Amish Style Graffiti

A curious custom developed at the Bontrager home during the 1880s. For some unexplained reason people began writing little messages on a plastered white wall in the attic, which at one time was an exterior wall because it was on an open porch. Signatures, pictures and poems eventually filled the whole space. The earliest is dated November 19, 1885 and reads:

"In this little lonely spot
I rite my name
Forgess me nat"
—Mattie Bontrager

In 1910 four girls signed their names to this:

"Leaves may wither
Flowers may die
Friends may forget you
But never will I."

A recent inscription reads:

"The Bontrager house
Held many a mouse.
So they set some traps
But the mice only smiled
And said, 'Perhaps.'"

Many of the writings are quite nonsensical but some are rather serious like this one:

"May your pathway be bright,
So it will if you do right,
And when life's journey is at an end,
May we all meet above
My dearly beloved friend."

John Bontrager, the Storyteller

Lame John Bontrager was also known as a gifted storyteller. When he took Fanny on shopping trips to nearby Middlebury, he usually waited outside on a bench and was soon engaged in swapping stories with the town men.

In later years Lame John added to his repertoire by traveling widely. It is said

The presence of a saddle suggests that not all horse travel is done with a buggy.

Pigs have been a part of the farm for many years and continue to provide income. A new hog house was constructed in 1990.

the railroad agent in Chicago knew him by name. No doubt many of his trips were spent visiting his widely scattered children and grandchildren. Of Lame John's nine children one moved to Michigan, one to Mississippi and later Oklahoma and three to Kansas. One son, Simon, contracted tuberculosis while living in Kansas. Lame John went out to help his son and family move back to Indiana. Simon died soon after his return. He was only 28.

Lame John officially retired in his 50s when son Daniel Bontrager took over the farm. John and Fanny moved into the *Dawdy Haus.* Lame John continued helping with the farm work as long as he was able and as long as things were not too modern. Accustomed to the old-style horse-drawn dump rake for raking hay, John took one look at son Daniel's new side delivery rake and promptly announced that henceforth Daniel would have to rake his own hay.

Lame John Bontrager died August 10, 1910. The family was gathered around his bed when he took his last breath. Before John died, he asked eleven-year-old grandson Gideon to come to him. Gideon had been a sickly boy and spent hours with his grandfather listening to his stories. John gave Gideon a hug and departed in death. Fanny Bontrager lived eight more years.

A Patriotic Predicament

John and Fanny Bontrager had nine children. Manasses, the child who rescued his toys from the house fire, went on to become a notable person in the Amish community. In 1895 he was ordained a minister in the Old Order Amish

A new milk house was built in 1977, but milk is still poured into milk cans and cooled with flowing water in a water trough.

An old-fashioned chicken house sheltering about 200 birds provides the family's eggs plus some to sell.

This barn provides shelter for the approximately 35 sheep on the farm when they are not out grazing.

church. In 1907 he and his family moved to a new Amish settlement in Ford County, Kansas, near Dodge City and in 1909 Manassas was ordained to the office of bishop.

During World War I Manasses wrote a letter to the *Sugarcreek Budget,* a weekly newspaper which published letters from far-flung Amish communities. In his letter Manasses encouraged young Amish men to stand their ground and not cooperate with the military. He also discouraged buying Liberty bonds. Several months later a United States marshal came to his Kansas farm, arrested Manasses Bontrager and escorted him to Cleveland, Ohio, where he and Samuel H. Smith, the editor of the *Budget,* were tried for espionage. The trial took place in Cleveland because the newspaper where the letter appeared was in that federal district. Smith and Bontrager were released without going to prison. They were each fined $500.

Manasses moved back to Indiana in 1921. Several years later he and his family again moved to a new Amish community at Sikeston, Missouri, where they remained until 1934. Manasses spent his last years near Centreville, Michigan, about 25 miles north of his boyhood home. A gifted writer, he once wrote a poem about growing up on the Bontrager-Miller farm.

The electric fence is powered by a 12-volt battery charged with a solar panel.

THE OLD HOME PLACE

There was a place I loved so dear
I called it home for many a year
No other place, to me, so grand
Whether far or near in this fair land.

When I came home there was father and mother
There were my sisters and my brother
No other place so dear to me
I had no care, I was so free.

I often think I yet can see
My footprints under the apple tree
But time has changed in many ways
The joys I had in childhood days.

How pleasant to think of days gone by
I cannot forget, don't ask me why
I love to think of my school days
So different from now in many ways.

And there were apples and also cherries
The huckleberry marsh so full of berries
And for what more could one wish
The lakes so near and full of fish.

When now I go, on the old home place
Of my boyhood dreams, I still can trace
Tho many a change, I now can see
But still it's next to home for me.

—M.E. Bontrager

The Barrens Bloom

When John and Fanny Bontrager first moved to their farm in New Pennsylvania, they found that the soil was not very productive. In fact, the area was also called "The Barrens." They did the best they could and were happy on the farm.

When son Daniel J. Bontrager took over the farm several years after his marriage to Lavina Mast in 1886, he made a concentrated effort to improve the quality of the soil. A faithful member of the Old Order Amish church, Daniel Bontrager was also a rather progressive farmer. He applied marl (a mixture containing carbonate of lime) and lime to his farm and rotated his crops with alfalfa. Eventually, neighboring farmers also adopted these methods, and while the area retained the name "The Barrens," it was no longer so bare.

(top) Corn is picked by hand in the field and shoveled onto the elevator where it is conveyed into the large corncrib.

(bottom) Many of the different farm implements used on the farm are housed in this large shed.

141

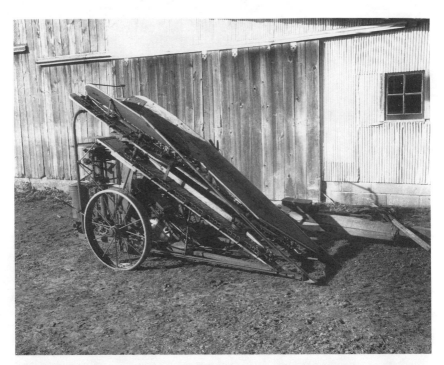

(top) The corn binder is used to gather corn stalks with the ears of corn attached, which are chopped up for the silo if they are green or put in shocks if they are dry.

(bottom) The husker-shredder is normally used for shredding dried corn stalks for fodder. If the ears of corn are left on the stalk, the machine husks the ears and separates them from the stalks and leaves.

(top) The tractor on the Bontrager-Miller farm has un-inflated rubber tires pulled over its steel wheels. The tractor provides power for a number of stationary pieces of equipment such as the ensilage cutter, the corn husker-shredder and the threshing machine.

(bottom) A team of Belgian horses pulls all farm implements through the fields.

In 1987 the Millers began growing sorghum on their farm. They convert it to molasses in this mill and sell directly from the farm.

Like many Amish farmers of his time, Daniel usually purchased new farm machinery as it became available. He generally tried to stay within the limits of the church *Ordnung*, but there were a few conflicts. Daniel Bontrager was one of the first Amish farmers in the area to buy a manure spreader. When some objection was made by the church leaders, he made the comment, "*Un fuss macha iva so stinkig un ding?*" (Why make a fuss about such a stinky thing?) He also went into partnership with a non-Amish person selling lime, something which was probably not fully approved by the church.

A man of above average intelligence and education, he had excelled in public spelling contests during his school years. For a few years before he was married, he even taught in a public school. In later years Daniel frequently offered advice in financial and legal matters to people in his community. He helped settle several estates, including some for non-Amish people.

Because of his considerable landholdings, he was sometimes called "Rich Dan." Even so, Daniel Bontrager was a quiet, kindly, mild-mannered man who was also deeply religious.

A Bad Year

Two incidents during the year 1908 tried the faith of the Bontrager family. One Sunday in the spring of the year, Daniel and Lavina and their six children were on the way to church when the two horses pulling the buggy began running out of control. When Daniel tried to swerve around another horse and buggy, the Bontrager vehicle upset into the ditch beside the road. The horses

Animal feed for the farm is ground here. The Millers also grind their own whole-wheat flour.

Ice for refrigeration is stored in this insulated ice house.

broke loose and continued running. Three-year-old Dannie broke his leg, and Lavina suffered a serious break of her elbow which left it permanently stiff.

Later, in the fall, a more serious accident involved Daniel and Lavina's son John Bontrager. Nineteen-year-old John was shredding fodder on a farm near Shipshewana. While feeding cornstalks into the shredder, he got his sleeve caught in the machine. His arm was torn off just below the shoulder. A local doctor called to the scene tied off the blood vessels with catgut. Miraculously, John survived and the wound healed although it took more than a year and the shoulder had to be dressed every morning.

John Bontrager went on to live a relatively normal life. He soon mastered such tasks as harnessing and driving horses and even learned to tie his shoes with only one arm. Like his grandfather, Lame John, he was also given a nickname related to his handicap. He became known as "One-Armed John." In 1916 he married Lizzie Helmuth. After she died during the flu epidemic of 1918, John married Lizzie's younger sister Katherine.

Then, in 1926 John nearly lost the use of his other arm. While helping to grind feed at the Bontrager-Miller farm, he caught his arm in the shaft of a motor. Badly mangled, it would probably have been amputated had there been another arm. A man with an incredibly strong constitution, John spent 45 days in the hospital and again recovered.

A Different Kind of Barn Raising

In 1909 Daniel Bontrager made a significant improvement to the barn on the Bontrager-Miller farm. Probably because the original barn had not been built by an Amish person, it was not a typical Pennsylvania bank barn, which provided ground level entrances to both the first and second floors. Daniel decided to alter the building.

When his father, Lame John, asked who was going to engineer the project and was told that Daniel himself would be in charge, he walked away silently shaking his head. A very large undertaking, indeed, Daniel Bontrager proved himself quite capable.

To accomplish the conversion the Bontrager barn had to be jacked up and placed on blocks. It was left in this precarious position over a Sunday when, of course, no work could be done. It is said that Daniel Bontrager's mind drifted from the sermon that day when it got a bit windy. A man named Mel Weaver was hired to pour cement walls around the barn, which took a total of 13 hours. After the walls were finished, earth was banked up to the second level on the north side of the barn, and Daniel Bontrager had his bank barn.

Trouble With Tractors

In addition to John Bontrager, another of Daniel and Lavina's sons also became well known in the Amish community. Jacob D. Bontrager moved onto the huckleberry farm after he married Fannie Schrock in 1909. Later, they moved to Clinton Township in neighboring Elkhart County where Jacob was ordained a minister in 1917 and a bishop in 1938. In the years immediately after World War II Jacob Bontrager was confronted with some difficult decisions concerning the acceptability of modern farm machinery. In his church district, Jacob permitted limited use of tractors in the fields. His decision was directly opposed to most other Amish leaders in the area. Eventually, all but one Amish district broke off relations with Jacob Bontrager's congregation. Jacob died in 1951.

Blocks of ice are cut from a nearby lake with this motorized saw. Ice harvesting is a community project involving several Amish families.

The following year his church district split, and the majority adopted cars and associated with the more liberal Beachy Amish Mennonites.

Adventure in the West

In 1894 word spread through the Elkhart-Lagrange Amish settlement that free land was available to homesteaders in North Dakota. The offer looked good to many young farmers who were suffering from the depression of the 1890s. By 1900 there were fifty Amish families living in Pierce and Rolette Counties, North Dakota. Most of the first settlers were young families with few if any children old enough to help with the harvest. They needed temporary farm hands. Four of Daniel J. Bontrager's sons answered this call from the west—Moses, Levi, Gideon and One-Armed John. Moses and Levi Bontrager liked North Dakota so well that they decided to stay. They were especially attracted to two of the daughters of Joseph Graber, an Amish farmer who had come to North Dakota in 1900 from Daviess County, Indiana. Levi Bontrager married Lizzie Graber in 1915 and Moses Bontrager married Lucy Graber in 1921.

Around 1925, after having lived in North Dakota several years, Moses and Lucy Bontrager decided to move back to Indiana. The North Dakota settlement declined rapidly during the depression of the 1930s. A few Amish families stayed until the 1950s.

Moses Bontrager Returns

When Moses and Lucy returned to Indiana, they settled on the Bontrager-Miller farm with their two small children. Over the next 14 years, they had six more children. At age 65 Daniel Bontrager had been doing all the farming and

A great deal of wood is needed to fuel the cooking and heating stoves. The Millers have an abundant supply from the acres of woodland on the farm.

148

A small gasoline engine powers a table saw in the workshop.

was no doubt glad for his son's return. However, Daniel continued helping with the farm work for nearly twenty more years.

Moses Bontrager made several notable improvements to the farm. During the 1930s, he added a corncrib and a silo and significantly increased the dairy herd from the six cows kept by his father, Daniel Bontrager. In those years milk was separated right on the farm. Mose Bontrager sold the cream and fed the skim milk to his hogs.

Mose and Lucy Bontrager's daughter Wilma, the current resident of the farm, remembers some features which have disappeared. Among these were a fruit drying stove which stood about 5 feet high, 3 feet wide and 2 feet deep. Manasses Bontrager's poem, "The Old Home Place," mentions fruit trees on the farm. There was also a smokehouse for curing meats and an outdoor bake oven. The oven was never used by Lucy Bontrager but her mother-in-law, Lavina Bontrager, had baked in it. Lavina kept a large tin box close to the bake oven where she collected ashes for making lye soap and for scrubbing aluminum cookware.

The Bontrager Farm Becomes the Miller Farm

Wilma, the youngest of the Moses and Lucy Bontrager children, married Roy Miller in 1960. The young couple took over the operation of the farm. At age 28 Roy was ordained to the ministry when the Middle Barrens District was divided into north and south districts because of increased population. The bishop resided in the south district and continued to oversee the north district. In 1972 Roy became bishop of the North Middle Barrens church district.

These martin houses lure the valuable, insect-eating birds to the Miller garden.

Twelve children were born to the Millers. Consequently, an addition was built to the house in 1979.

Moses and Lucy Bontrager lived in the *Dawdy Haus* during their last years. Moses died in 1982 and Lucy died in 1988. After Lucy's death, Roy's widowed mother moved into the *Dawdy Haus*.

A Close Call

In 1972 the Miller family escaped without serious injury when the house once again caught fire. One evening while Wilma was lighting a gasoline pressure lamp, she noticed that the cap was leaking air. She turned off the flame immediately, but when she opened the filler cap, the lamp sprayed flames, lighting her clothing. She quickly extinguished her clothing preventing serious burns, but the lamp burned out of control. A jug of kerosene used for a non-electric iron ignited. A vinyl tablecloth also caught fire, but the Millers managed to bring the flames under control with fire extinguishers before the firemen came. However, the wooden ceiling was badly charred, and the house was so smoky that the children had to sleep at the homes of neighbors for a time.

A Diversified Farm

The 223-acre Bontrager-Miller farm, is somewhat typical of American family farms of a half century or more ago. In this respect it is somewhat unusual today, even among the Amish, especially in the Elkhart-LaGrange settlement.

The Miller family currently (1991) milks 19 Holstein cows by hand and the milk is placed in old-style metal cans and cooled in water. A truck picks up the milk cans and takes them to a cheese house between Shipshewana and Middlebury.

In addition to dairy cows, they also have a hog operation, 30 to 35 sheep, about 200 laying hens and more than a dozen free-roaming silky bantam chickens. In 1991 over 200 mallard ducklings were hatched on the farm.

Roy Miller cuts his hay with a ground-driven sickle bar mower and picks it up loose in the field with an old-fashioned hay loader. Roy has always used a machine similar to a silo filler to blow chopped hay into the barn's haymows.

Ear corn is picked by hand. Arranged in shocks, the corn stalks dry in the field and are fed through a shredder to make corn fodder. Corn for ensilage is harvested with a ground-driven corn binder and fed into a motor-driven silo filler (ensilage cutter). Along with several neighboring families, the Millers belong to a silo filling ring which shares both work and equipment necessary to this task.

The Millers also belong to a wheat and oats threshing ring. The threshing machine currently used came from Wisconsin. Very few northern Indiana Amish farmers still grow wheat. Generally not profitable for a small farmer, the Millers grind their own wheat into flour. They bag the whole wheat flour and sell it directly to a growing number of local customers.

Quite unusual for the area, the Millers also grow sorghum and have their own mill for making molasses. The sorghum stalks, stripped of their leaves and heads, are pressed to extract the juice. This liquid is cooked and the impurities skimmed off until a thick molasses is formed. Begun in 1987, this new venture has proved quite successful.

The windmill is no longer used to pump water. A diesel engine now serves this purpose.

Old-Style Refrigeration

Unlike many Amish in the area who use kerosene-operated refrigerators, the Millers still refrigerate with ice. In the early 1900s ice was typically harvested from lakes and stored in a community ice house. In later years a local company made periodic ice deliveries directly to the farms. Moses Bontrager and Roy Miller bought ice from one of these vendors for many years. When the company found it could no longer profitably continue the ice routes, it abruptly stopped. The Millers and some other nearby Amish reverted to the old way and began harvesting ice from a nearby lake.

Each year they gather for an ice harvesting frolic. Roy Miller saws the ice with a motorized circular saw. The blocks of ice are stored in individual ice houses on the farms. During his years on the Bontrager-Miller farm, Moses Bontrager had built a simple ice house which he insulated with sawdust. Today, it has styrofoam insulation and is still used to store ice.

To provide refrigeration the ice is placed in an old-fashioned metal ice box similar to those found in North American homes in the 1930s. Some food is also cooled on the enclosed porch in what the Millers call a *Wasser Haus*. Here well water runs through a series of enclosed rectangular tanks on its way to the supply tank. This arrangement was originally used to obtain drinking water and to cool milk in cans.

A hand-dug, forty-foot deep well on the porch was used until the 1960s. Today, a well just outside the house, pumped with a diesel engine, provides water for the family and the farm animals. A windmill on its tall tower still stands by the well but it is no longer used.

The Miller family uses wood as the main source of energy for heat and cooking. However, during the summer a kerosene burning cookstove is used because it generates less heat and may easily be turned on and off.

According to a study done by a professor at nearby Goshen College, only about thirty percent of the Amish in the Elkhart-LaGrange settlement are farmers. Many Amish wage earners in the area work in mobile home factories. Despite this trend, the Roy Miller family has maintained an old-fashioned diversified farm.

Residents of the Indiana Farm

1. 1862   John J. Bontrager IV (1834-1910)
   Fanny Kauffman (1834-1918)
   > Born in Somerset County, Pennsylvania
   > Moved to Indiana with parents in 1844
2. 1888   Daniel J. Bontrager (1860-1946)
   Lavina Mast (1866-1950)
   > Son of John IV and Fanny Bontrager
3. 1925   Moses Bontrager (1896-1982)
   Lucy J. Graber (1902- 1988)
   > Son of Daniel and Lavina Bontrager
4. 1960   Roy W. Miller (1940-)
   Wilma M. Bontrager (1939-)
   > Daughter of Moses and Lucy Bontrager

Readings and Sources

Beiler, Katie, ed. *Descendants and History of Christian Fisher (1757-1838).* Soudersburg, Pennsylvania: Eby's Quality Printing, 1988.

Bird-in-Hand 1734-1984: A History of Bird-in-Hand, Pennsylvania, 1984.

Bontrager, Sonja. "The Memory Wall," *Heritage Country,* Vol.8, No.1 (Spring and Summer 1987), 44-45.

Coffee, Brian. "Nineteenth-Century Barns of Geauga County, Ohio," *Pioneer America,* Vol.10, No.2 (December 1978), 53-63.

Dornbusch, Charles H. and John K. Heyl. *Pennsylvania German Barns.* Allentown, Pennsylvania: Pennsylvania German Folklore Society, 1956.

Dyck, Cornelius, ed. *An Introduction to Mennonite History.* Scottdale, Pennsylvania: Herald Press, 1967.

Ensminger, Robert F. "A Search for the Origin of the Pennsylvania Barn," *Pennsylvania Folklife,* Vol.30, No.2 (Winter 1980-81), 50-71.

Erb, Henry L. "The Christian Schlabach Family Comes to America," *Heritage Review,* Vol.1 (December 1990), 4-9.

Friesen, Steve. *A Modest Mennonite Home.* Intercourse, Pennsylvania: Good Books, 1990.

Glass, Joseph W. *The Pennsylvania Culture Region: A View from the Barn.* Ann Arbor, Michigan: UMI Research Press, 1986.

Glassie, Henry. "Eighteenth-Century Cultural Process in Delaware Valley Folk Building," *Winterthur Portfolio,* 7 (1972), 29-57.

_____. *Patterns in the Material Folk Culture of the Eastern United States.* Philadelphia, Pennsylvania: University of Pennsylvania Press, 1969.

Good, Merle. *Who Are The Amish?* Intercourse, Pennsylvania: Good Books, 1985.

_____ and Phyllis. *Twenty Most Asked Questions about the Amish and Mennonites.* Lancaster, Pennsylvania: Good Books, 1979.

History of LaGrange County, Indiana. Chicago: F.A. Battery and Company, 1882.

Hostetler, John A. *Amish Society.* Baltimore, Maryland: Johns Hopkins University Press, 1980.

Kaufman, Stanley A. *Germanic Folk Culture in Eastern Ohio.* Walnut Creek, Ohio: German Culture Museum, 1986.

_____ and Leroy Beachy. *Amish in Eastern Ohio.* Walnut Creek, Ohio: German Culture Museum, 1991.

Kauffman, Henry J. *The American Farmhouse.* New York: Hawthorn, 1975.

Kollmorgen, Walter M. *Culture of a Contemporary Rural Community: The Old Order Amish of Lancaster County, Pennsylvania.* Washington D.C.: U.S. Department of Agriculture, Rural Life Studies, 1942.

Kraybill, Donald B. *The Riddle of Amish Culture.* Baltimore, Maryland: Johns Hopkins University Press, 1988.

_____ . The Puzzles of Amish Life. Intercourse, Pennsylvania: Good Books, 1990.

Gingerich, Hugh F. and Rachel W. Kreider. *Amish and Amish Mennonite Genealogies.* Gordonville, Pennsylvania: Pequea Publishers, 1986.

Long, Amos Jr. *The Pennsylvania German Family Farm.* Breinigsville, Pennsylvania: The Pennsylvania German Society, 1972.

Luthy, David. *The Amish in America: Settlements That Failed, 1840-1960.* Aylmer, Ontario: Pathway Publishers, 1986.

Meyors, Thomas J. "Population Growth and Its Consequences in the Elkhart-LaGrange Old Order Amish Settlement," *Mennonite Quarterly Review,* Vol. 65, No. 3 (July 1991), pp. 308-321.

Noble, Allen G. *Wood, Brick and Stone: The North American Landscape, Vol.1: Houses, Vol.2: Barns and Farm Structures.* Amherst, Massachusetts: The University of Massachusetts Press, 1984.

Scott, Stephen E. *The Amish Wedding and Other Special Occasions of the Old Order Communities.* Intercourse, Pennsylvania: Good Books, 1988.

_____ . *Plain Buggies. Intercourse, Pennsylvania: Good Books, 1981.*

_____ and Kenneth R. Pellman. Living Without Electricity. Intercourse, Pennsylvania: Good Books, 1990.

Shoemaker, Alfred I. *The Pennsylvania Barn.* Kutztown, Pennsylvania: Pennsylvania Folklife Society, 1959.

Stoltzfus, Nicholas, comp. *Nonresistance Put to Test.* Aylmer, Ontario: Pathway Publishers, 1981.

Swank, Scott T. *Arts of the Pennsylvania Germans.* New York: W.W. Norton, 1983.

Two-Hundredth Anniversary 1754-1954, Intercourse, Pennsylvania. Intercourse, Pennsylvania: Intercourse Civic Association, 1954.

Weaver, William Woys. "The Pennsylvania German House: European Antecedents and New World Forms," *Winterthur Portfolio,* Vol.21, No.4 (Winter 1986), 243-264.

Wilhelm, Hubert G. H. and Michael Miller. "Half-Timber Construction: A Relic Building Method in Ohio," *Pioneer America,* Vol.IV, No.2 (July 1974), 43-51.

Yoder, Edna O. and Marion G. Bontrager. *Descendants of John J. Bontrager IV and Fanny Kauffman 1834-1980.* Middlebury, Indiana, 1980.

Yoder, Joe D. and Henry L. Erb. *Descendants of Daniel D. Swartzentruber Jr. 1842-1988.* Gordonville, Pennsylvania: Gordonville Print Shop, 1988.

Yoder, Paton. *Eine Wuertzel: Tennessee John Stoltzfus.* Lititz, Pennsylvania: Sutter House, 1979.

_____ . *Tradition and Transition: Amish Mennonites and Old Order Amish 1800-1900.* Scottdale, Pennsylvania: Herald Press, 1991.

About the Author

Stephen E. Scott grew up in southwestern Ohio. In his youth, he became impressed with the life of the plain people. He subsequently visited various Amish, Mennonite and Brethren groups in Ohio. Eventually, he also worked, lived and worshiped in several of the communities.

In 1969 Scott moved to Lancaster County, Pennsylvania, where he became a member of the Old Order River Brethren, a group related to the Amish and Mennonites.

Scott studied at Cedarville (Ohio) College. He is the author of *Plain Buggies*, *Why Do They Dress That Way?* and *The Amish Wedding*. He is also coauthor of *Living Without Electricity*.

Scott married Harriet Sauder in 1973. They have three children and live near Columbia, Pennsylvania. He works as a researcher for The People's Place and Good Books in Intercourse, Pennsylvania.